TRUE WEALTH

TRUE WEALTH

The GUIDE Process for Finding and
Financing Your Ideal Life

ISBN   978-1-5445-1456-7   Paperback
      978-1-5445-1616-5   Ebook

THE GUIDE PROCESS FOR FINDING AND
FINANCING YOUR IDEAL LIFE

True Wealth

MARK CLURE

CONTENTS

For my wife and best friend, Robin, and my kids, Casey, Cody, and Carey

For my grandkids, Kristen, Skylar, Kyla, Liam, Davis, and Baby C

And for all of you out there who have never stopped searching:

May you realize your purpose and unleash your full potential.

INTRODUCTION

As a kid I loved to play football. After high school, the University of Oklahoma offered me a scholarship. I was selected to the Big Eight All-Conference team and ultimately by the Washington Redskins.

It's a great story, but it's not true. It was eight-year-old me's vision of the future.

Eight-year-old me had also figured a few things out. I knew that I loved learning and exploring new places and ideas. And I knew that somehow I was destined for something bigger.

My inner explorer has led me to try some "out of the ordinary" activities. Swimming with sharks, cliff skiing, bungee jumping, and "surfing" a Class 5 river to name a few. Naturally, when visiting Maui, I arranged a guided sea kayak trip in an aquatic nature preserve that featured a big lava bowl full of sunshine and amazing snorkeling. But you couldn't get there by a motorboat. You couldn't hike there (at least not legally). You definitely couldn't drive there. You could only reach the preserve by kayak. Right up my alley.

My wife and I shared a two-person kayak. Another family joined us—a father, daughter, and son. Paul was about forty-five years old, Amy twenty, and Ben seventeen. The father and son shared one kayak; Amy had her own.

While he still had one foot on dry land, Paul fell out of the kayak as he tried to board before we launched. On the water he was incapable of paddling. I could see he was completely out of his element; he had no business on the water. He was a really nice guy, but kayaking was not his strong suit, so the son had to paddle and steer.

We kayaked to the spot we were looking for and had it all to ourselves. We beached the kayaks and snorkeled in perhaps the most beautiful place I've ever snorkeled in my life. The water was crystal clear, and it was so quiet we could hear the fish crunching on the coral.

We got back in our kayaks to continue up the coastline. The guide warned us that around the next corner there was a point where the wind and waves come up a lot, creating a potentially treacherous situation. He advised us to stay close to shore. One after another, we went around the corner. Amy was out in front, and then my wife and me, and then the dad and son, followed by the guide.

Amy strayed too far from the shore, and the current started carrying her out into the ocean. She quickly panicked in what felt like a life-or-death situation, trying to row while screaming in fear with tears rolling down her cheeks.

I paddled our kayak as close to her as I could to try to comfort and communicate with her. But the further out we went, the more dangerous it became. The winds blew at forty miles an hour, and the white caps were up to five feet high. Imagine being in the kayak at water level, with a five-foot wave in front of you—we could barely see where we were going.

I kept within twenty feet of Amy, but then my wife began panicking in our kayak, too. I tried to calm the both of them, but Amy was so panicked she was unable to paddle. Her kayak drifted farther out to sea, pushed by the wind and waves.

You would have expected the guide to step up, take control, and get us to safety. Instead, he completely panicked as well. He was checked out, frustrated, and began yelling at all of us. Although I'm not an expert kayaker, I remained calm and took over directing the group.

Then a wave lifted our kayak, and, when we smacked down from the swell, the kayak flipped, and my seat broke away from the kayak on one side. Fortunately, we were able to get back into the kayak and paddle, but without my seat attached properly, which provides leverage and power, I didn't have the force I needed to rescue Amy myself. The guide hooked the father and son to the back of our kayak and then went out to get Amy.

With Paul and Ben attached to us, I could hear Ben say, "Dad, I'm going to get us out of this. We're going to make it." He may not have known it at the time, but that was a life-changing moment for Ben.

The guide returned, attached Amy to the front of our boat and himself in the lead, making a four-kayak chain. The guide pulled from the front, I pulled from the middle, and Ben pulled like his life depended on it. We were so exhausted that we really weren't making much headway against a really strong current.

Through the waves, we noticed that a crowd of about twenty people had gathered on the shore, watching us struggle and fight for our lives. We later learned that they had been debating calling the Coast Guard.

Out of the crowd, one man got in his kayak, paddled out, and connected to us. He provided the additional power we needed to land the boats.

We were all safe. Everybody was shaken up and exhausted, but it was a pretty memorable event for me. My wife's view of the trip—and I believe the other family's as well, or at least Amy's—is that we'd have all been in big trouble if I hadn't remained calm in that crisis.

That Nagging Feeling

By now you might be wondering what kayaking has to do with True Wealth...or finding and financing your ideal life. That experience provided a key piece to the puzzle of what makes me...me. Ultimately, it led me to understand why I'm a financial planner and writing this book.

That feeling of calm in a crisis was familiar. It wasn't something I had trained for, or ever thought about. It was in me! While others around me panic, I don't simply stay calm. I KNOW we'll be okay. Not hope, not just believe—KNOW.

I realized that throughout my life in times of crisis, I am overcome by an inner calm and peacefulness. When I spoke to friends, they consistently told me that I make them feel secure and confident to try things they would have never tried. As a result of getting outside of their comfort zones, they've had personal breakthroughs and have grown as people.

When I returned home from Maui, I thought through the kayak experience and spent a lot of time evaluating my past, looking at sections of early childhood, adolescence, teenage years, into my twenties and thirties, in an attempt to discover more of what makes me who I am.

Themes started to emerge from earlier periods in my life. The pieces started to come together.

Lighting the Fire

I began close to home to find meaning in my life by focusing on my family. As my children and grandchildren started to grow up, I provided emotional and financial support, trying to positively impact their obvious talents. My wife and I encouraged them to explore new ideas, places, and opportunities that supported all they could become, by spending time with them and providing extraordinary academic and athletic training.

As an example, through her hard work, our oldest granddaughter was accepted into an Oxford University program during high school, and we were able to cover the cost of the program. The experience had an enormous impact on her life. She describes this time as finding her people. She met lifelong friends from around the world and gained significant academic confidence that has carried her throughout college.

I wanted to give my children and grandchildren an advantage with the things they were good at already, to somehow enhance their situations and help them become part of the 15 percent of people who love what they do. When I saw the results, I expanded my scope and started looking toward what I could do for others. That change involved actively searching for my purpose, and ultimately developing The GUIDE Process, the path to achieving True Wealth.

My dad, I'm sorry to say, left an important dream unfulfilled. He worked as an air traffic controller and trainer of controllers, and eventually, he worked his way up to manage several air traffic control centers across the U.S. My dad never asked me for anything or told me what was important to him until he was near death. A week before he died, my dad asked me to have him cremated and to send his ashes to the moon. I suppose I'll never know for sure, but I think he really wanted to be an astronaut. Today, some of his ashes reside on the moon. Although he never fulfilled this dream during his life, I helped him achieve it following his death. I want to help you achieve your dream and True Wealth in this lifetime.

Getting What You Need

The Rolling Stones sing "You Can't Always Get What You Want." Sorry Mick, but I believe it's more like this: When people get what they want, it's not always what they need—especially when it comes to career and lifestyle.

According to studies, 85 percent of people don't like what they do for a living. I'd say even more. Most people work only to support the things they'd really like to do. They get through their day rather than gaining something from it. And 98 percent never accomplish the things that are most important to them.

Maybe you're in the 85 percent and are thinking that you need to make a change in your life, but you don't know how. You feel your life could be better, but you don't have a process to discover what your ideal life might look like or how you would be able to support your family in moving to an ideal life.

Imagine if you could light the fire that enables you to work on something truly meaningful and change the world. Imagine if you were in the small percentage of people who love their jobs and feel that they are making a difference in the world.

It happened for me. And it can happen for you.

If you:

- Are struggling to find your purpose in life

- Have found your purpose but aren't living it

- Find yourself with work that's not fulfilling

- Need to make a change

- Are a student deciding what you'd like to do with your life

- Have accumulated wealth and want to make a bigger impact on the world

- Have an idea of your purpose and want to refine it

- Are a financial advisor looking for a more meaningful connection with clients

- Are a consultant or coach whose purpose is to help others

- Are a financial advisor seeking a unique niche

This book is for you!

Three Parts to Achieving True Wealth

I've been a financial advisor for twenty-five years. When asked in an initial meeting what it is that people would like to accomplish, 99 percent of those still working said they wanted "to retire." And when? "As soon as possible."

But only one in four actually completed a plan, let alone achieved the goal of retiring. So, I started asking a different question: Is there anything that you've always wanted to do that you haven't yet accomplished?

It was a game changer. What had been a 25 percent completion rate on financial plans became virtually 100 percent. Rather than moving away from a negative situation—a job they didn't really enjoy—clients were moving toward something meaningful to them, a dream they hadn't fulfilled. On the way to fulfilling that dream we'd work on getting them retired as well. People need a process with an exciting end result.

Here are the three pieces to living an ideal life and achieving True Wealth.

1. Redefining wealth as what's most important to you, and how you can use it to help others. True Wealth is *always* about more than money.

2. Creating an exciting goal rather than simply moving away from a negative situation.

3. Discovering your life's purpose and unlocking your potential.

I struggled with a lack of full knowledge regarding my purpose and potential for a long time, although I had bits and pieces of it. It took me close to twenty years to figure it out, but now I have a process to do it much more quickly.

I've cracked the code to finding it.

That's what The GUIDE Process is about.

The GUIDE Process

The GUIDE Process can take six days or six months, but you will get it done if you follow the process I've set out in this book.

As I stated earlier, it took me a long time to figure things out. I searched for years for a process, but there wasn't one out there. I found a bunch of nice quotes like "Do what you love, and you'll never work a day in your life." That's wonderful advice, but how?

Four or five years ago, I came across a book called *Start with Why* by Simon Sinek, which influenced me and got me thinking about The GUIDE Process. He also has a video on YouTube called "How Great Leaders Inspire Action." He created what he calls the Golden Circle as a means for a business to discover its purpose. The Golden Circle looks like a target with the outside circle representing "What," the middle circle representing "How," and the central circle, or the target area, representing "Why." The way he described it is that all businesses know what they do. And many of them know how they do it. But very few know why. He states, people don't buy *what* you do or *how* you do it. However, they will buy *why* you do it. And he backed his process up by using the scientific function of the brain.

I could see how Sinek's Golden Circle would work for a business, but it was less useful in helping me find my personal purpose.

I turned to the process I knew best—the financial planning process. Step One—Gather current financial information: income, spending, and assets; Step Two—Create financial goals; Step Three—Identify and evaluate options and alternatives; Step Four—Create a written plan; Step Five—Evaluate and revise.

I then converted this process to The GUIDE Process, which follows the same format. So,

1. Step One became **G**ather information about your past. Your personal history.

2. Step Two became **U**nlock your potential and create your ideal future.

3. Step Three became **I**dentify the themes that are uniquely you.

4. Step Four became **D**evelop your purpose statement.

5. Step Five became **E**valuate and evolve.

After using this process for myself and clients, I'm ready to show you how to use it, too.

How The GUIDE Process Works

If you follow The GUIDE Process you will have a clear path to acquiring True Wealth. There are two parts to this book—personal and financial—that consist of step-by-step processes to uncover your purpose and to put together a plan that will allow you to live your ideal life.

The first part is The GUIDE for Life Purpose. Here, you will start by answering questions regarding events from various stages of your life that have impacted you. The results of this process will yield themes that will reveal your purpose and enable you to describe it to others. Once you know your purpose, decisions become easier, and you will know what you need to do in order to achieve your potential. In this section you will create a personal purpose statement that defines who you are, what you do, and how you will make a difference in the world. (If you already know your purpose but don't know how to finance it, you can skip The GUIDE for Life Purpose, and move onto The GUIDE for Finances.)

I'm sure you're thinking you have to pay the power bill and put groceries on the table. That's where The GUIDE to Finance comes in. It will enable you to identify and prioritize the significant differences between your current and ideal life. You'll learn how much money you need to live your ideal life, where that money's coming from, and if you need to make a significant change in your life in order to finance it and to achieve True Wealth.

As you go through this process, you may uncover new and exciting things that you didn't know about yourself. You may even feel a new enthusiasm for life.

For me, helping others find True Wealth is exciting. But instead of focusing on using my knowledge to help my existing clients, I decided to write this book to widen the scope of those who can benefit from it. In addition, I'm building a workforce of financial advisors who use The GUIDE Process, which is also exciting. I know what I'm working toward— helping people around the world acquire True Wealth—and that gives me the energy, focus, and clarity of purpose that I didn't have before.

Do you know what you're working toward?

Let's explore the meaning of True Wealth and then begin the process that allows you to create it.

PART I

The **GUIDE** for Life Purpose

MOVING TOWARD POSITIVE GOALS AND UNCOVERING YOUR LIFE'S PURPOSE

CHAPTER 1

Acquiring True Wealth

My client Rich Voyd[1] was a good car salesman. People liked him, he was friendly, and he made a decent living. But because he wasn't that interested in cars, Rich didn't love his job, and he'd spend his days looking forward to quitting time.

Rich's true love was raising racehorses. He did everything he could to give his horses the best shot at winning, such as hauling them from place to place in order to avoid harsh winters and poor feeding grounds, which enabled Rich's horses to continue training and to remain strong and fast. However, because of his job, Rich had limited time to spend with his horses, leaving him feeling unfulfilled and frustrated.

In searching for a way to merge his passion with his skills, Rich landed a job as a sales manager for a horse trailer company. Instead of spending his days looking forward to quitting time like he had while at the car dealership, Rich now wanted to work. He quickly became National Sales Manager. Attending horse races, rodeos, and other horse events and developing relationships with racehorse owners was part of his job. He was in his element with people who loved what he loved. And he had more time to spend with his own racehorses.

As a result of forging relationships with other racehorse owners and learning of their needs for transporting racehorses in a more comfortable environment, Rich convinced his company to

---

1   The name and details of this story have been changed to protect the privacy of the individual involved;
    however, the story illustrates the point of what happened.

improve its horse trailers. Over the years, the trailers continued to improve, and the horses that used the trailers won more races than they had in the past, resulting in increased sales for Rich's company and turning it into one of the largest selling high-end trailer companies in the United States.

Not only did Rich love his job, but his income jumped from approximately $50,000 a year as a car salesman to several million dollars a year as the national sales manager. Although Rich was always a happy guy, he was so much happier when working with racehorses and with the horse trailer company. His fulfillment level went through the roof, and he accomplished more than he thought he ever would.

Moving Toward Positive Goals

By moving toward a positive goal—wanting to work with racehorses—rather than toward a negative goal—wanting to quit his car salesman job, Rich found what I call True Wealth. He had personal fulfillment and financial security.

Most people, however, get stuck in setting negative goals and don't think about a positive one. According to a University of Scranton study,[2] fewer than 25 percent of those who make New Year's resolutions are still committed to their goal as of February 1, and only 8 percent accomplish their goal. That's because New Year's resolutions are typically negative goals, and negative goals lead us to focus on the very thing we're trying to avoid, such as losing weight or quitting smoking.

Moving toward a negative goal leads to stress, depression, decreased self-esteem, and decreased life satisfaction. In addition, it hinders your ability to think positively about achieving your goals.

If your thoughts and behaviors are aligned with your beliefs, your values, and your expectations—if you move toward positive goals—then you'll feel positive about your life. You'll also have a greater chance of accomplishing your goals and achieving True Wealth.

Changing the Life Planning Process

Reaching financial goals is no different: people set a goal for retirement to escape their current negative situation instead of making a plan for a positive outcome. This means financial planning is not compelling for most people; they don't know how to do it and they don't think they will ever have enough money to achieve their goals anyway. Therefore, many don't complete the financial planning process. However, statistics show that those who create financial plans will have more money, income, and net worth than those who don't create financial plans.

As I mentioned, 99 percent of those who come in to see me for financial planning advice state they "want to retire as soon as possible." Unlike Rich, who moved toward a positive goal of working with racehorses, many clients want to move toward a negative goal of not working. They want to retire, but don't know their purpose, what they want to do once they retire, how much retirement will cost, or when they can retire.

---

2   John Norcross, "Auld Lang Syne; Success Predictors, Change Processes, and Self-Reported Outcomes," *Journal of Clinical Psychology* 8, no. 4 (April 2002): 397–405.

MARK CLURE

Vacation planning is the opposite of retirement planning. When planning a vacation, you know when you're leaving, where you're going, what you're going to do when you get there, when you'll come home, and how you'll pay for the trip.

You can change the life and financial planning process so that it's just as exciting as the vacation planning process by moving toward a positive goal, such as working with racehorses, rather than toward a negative goal, such as retiring.

Redefining Wealth

If you Google the word "wealth," you'll see it defined as an "abundance of valuable possessions." The word is derived from the Old English word "well," which meant well-being and prosperity.

Having wealth is often not enough to make people happy. There are many examples of unhappy and dissatisfied, rich and famous people such as Howard Hughes and Marilyn Monroe. In addition, numerous lottery winners state their lives were ruined by their new-found monetary wealth. They lost friends and weren't able to trust people; some were the target of hitmen hired to kill them so that relatives could gain control of their money. Clearly money isn't everything. What good is an enormous pile of money if you're unhappy with your life?

Two of the highest-paying occupations in the United States, probably worldwide, are dentist and lawyer. According to the Center for Disease Control,[3] dentists are two and a half times more likely to die by suicide than the average population. Fifty-two percent of lawyers are dissatisfied with their lives.

Ed Diener, a psychologist from the University of Utah, conducted a comparative study of life satisfaction among the *Forbes* 400 richest Americans and an indigenous semi-nomadic tribe in east Africa that had no power or running water. On a scale of one to seven, the billionaires scored an average of 5.8 in life satisfaction versus 5.7 for the tribespeople, and three of the ten on the Forbes list scored less than average.[4]

In the movie *Jerry Maguire*, Jerry is a very successful sports agent who, although he is rich, hates himself and what his life has become. He decides to find his purpose in life. Jerry's mentor, Dickey Fox, who's also a sports agent, says, "Look, I don't have all the answers in life, to be honest I've failed as often as I've succeeded, but I love my wife, I love my life, and I wish you my kind of success." Which Jerry ultimately goes on to achieve.

The framers of the U.S. Constitution and the Declaration of Independence got it right when they wrote that we have certain unalienable rights, including the pursuit of happiness. But they weren't the first to state that. More than 2,300 years ago Aristotle said, "Happiness is the ultimate end and purpose of human existence."

---

3   Elizabeth Brown, "Are Dentists Really More Prone to Suicide?," Vice Media Group, March 28, 2017, *https://www.vice.com/en_us/article/5344jz/are-dentists-really-more-prone-to-suicide.*

4   Ed Diener and Martin Seligman, "Beyond Money," *American Psychological Journal*, 2004.

In order to be happy, we need a new definition of wealth. Instead of looking at wealth as how much money or material possessions you have, think of it as articulating your unique purpose in life and unlocking your potential so you can live a life that you love, have the means to support it, and positively affect the lives of others. That's what I call True Wealth.

Tragedy Leads to Change

Glen Dillon[5] is another example of someone who redefined wealth. He's a filmmaker in his early fifties, married with one daughter, and runs the marketing division of a large software company in the San Francisco Bay Area, everything from administration to content development to dealing with a staff of hundreds. It's a demanding and exhausting job, but it pays well. Because he works long hours, Glen is wiped out by the grind and is unable to do the things he loves after work, such as mountain biking, skateboarding, or back country skiing.

Last year, Glen witnessed his friend ski off a cliff and die. Glen tried to revive him but, despite his emergency medical training, he failed. He couldn't save him. Between the trauma Glen experienced after his friend's death and the pressure at work, Glen knew he had to make a change in his life, one that enabled him to do something he loved while continuing to support his family. But working in the software industry was the only type of work he'd ever done.

Glen and I reevaluated his definition of wealth, and together we're working through The GUIDE Process so that Glen can discover his purpose, put it into action, and acquire True Wealth. Because he loves outdoor recreation, such as kayaking and back country skiing, and because he possesses a great deal of skill and passion in cinematography, I envision him setting up a business that combines those skills, some kind of adventure filmmaking company and possibly an emergency medical kit for outdoor enthusiasts. Instead of spending his days at a marketing division and feeling unfulfilled, Glen will be able to spend more time doing what he loves. I'm excited I can help him make that change in his life.

People with a Purpose Get It Done

If you have a purpose and know what you really want to do, you have a better chance of getting it done. Your purpose helps you stay focused and enables you to make decisions more easily. Purpose provides the passion that'll drive you to extraordinary lengths to achieve your positive goals. Purpose and passion give you the energy you need to succeed.

If you can't see what you're working toward, if you don't know your purpose, it's like trying to build a puzzle without a picture on the box. Knowing your purpose gives you part of the picture, which allows you to put the pieces together to complete the puzzle and fulfill your purpose.

---

5   The name and details of this story have been changed to protect the privacy of the individual involved; however, the story illustrates the point of what happened.

Two Graduates of the School of Purpose

Two men, Mark Foster and Dean Taylor, also found their purpose and ultimately True Wealth as a result of redefining wealth.

Mark is eighty-eight years old, active, a volunteer, philanthropist, and a fabulous guy. When you ask him, "Hey, how are you?" he enthusiastically says "Fantastic" 100 percent of the time. His attitude and enthusiasm make people smile and feel better about their day. I asked him if he ever says he's fantastic even when he's not. He replied, "Sometimes I have to lie to myself, but it raises the ceiling on how my day and my life turn out. Instead of things turning out all right, they'll turn out fantastic." Mark achieves True Wealth by positively affecting others' lives and by spreading joy.

Dean achieves True Wealth in a similar manner. When someone asks Dean how he's doing, he always says, "I'm blessed." Half of the people respond with "Me too," 40 percent say, "I like that," and the rest say, "Well good for you, but I don't know about me." To that last group, Dean says, "You are. We all are. You just don't know it yet." Dean receives positive responses from all three groups, but the last group, those he tells are blessed, "lights up more than the others." And that "lights" him up too. To Dean, that is wealth, and the sense of fulfillment he gets from it gives him True Wealth.

As you can see, you need to define wealth in your own terms. What does wealth mean to you? How will you be happy and fulfilled? What's your purpose? Once you know your purpose and are able to articulate it, you attract people who either benefit from or share the same view. That's where things start to transform your life in a positive way and lead to acquiring True Wealth.

There Is a Process to Discover Your Life's Purpose

By now you're probably asking yourself: How do I find my life's purpose? It seems so difficult.

You can and will find it. The GUIDE for Life Purpose will walk you through the process.

This process worked for me and works for my clients.

I discovered that my purpose is "to help others find their purpose and unlock their potential, so that together we can unleash the full power of all human potential." When I test-drove it on a few people, they said, "Oh yeah, that's you."

While implementing my purpose in small ways within my family, I also wrestled with differentiating myself from other financial planners. When someone asked, "So what do you do?" and I said I was a financial planner or a financial advisor, they changed the subject or pulled out a book. Occasionally, they would talk about "the market." It wasn't a conversation starter. But if I said, "I'm Mark Clure, a partner at Enso Wealth Management, and we specialize in helping clients achieve their ideal life," it changed the game. It was a conversation starter. But once you say that, you have to be able to do it. That got me thinking and, ultimately, writing this book was part of my purpose. Showing you the process to discover your purpose, live your ideal life, and achieve True Wealth excites me. I constantly have ideas; I even wake up with ideas, jump out of bed, and run to write them down.

I want you to get excited about discovering your life's purpose too. Your experience is probably going to be different than the examples I provided, but as you work through this book you will see how The GUIDE Process can help you find purpose and meaning in your life that will carry you through to the end.

CHAPTER 2

G: Gather Information

A 2014 STUDY IN *PSYCHOLOGICAL SCIENCE*[6] FOUND THAT PEOPLE WHO HAD A DEFINED PURPOSE LIVED on average eight years longer, regardless of the purpose. In the *Journal of Research in Personality*,[7] people who have purpose are more likely to save money and to make investments that support their life's goals. The MIDUS study[8] states that people with a purpose have a 39 percent greater net worth and a 13 percent higher income than those who don't have a purpose.

Ed Pecis discovered his purpose after working for decades as a sheriff in California on an anti-drug and crime beat. It was pretty dangerous work with brutally demanding hours. Ed was really good at his job, but found that interactions with criminals and suspects often clashed with his Christian values. He felt a strong spiritual calling, so he shifted his job and became ordained as a church deacon. The conflict between those two worlds is astounding. Realizing that people whom he once thought of as scumbags were "somebody's children" changed Ed's whole worldview.

---

6   P. Hill and N. Turiano. "Purpose in Life as a Predictor of Mortality," *Psychological Science* 25, no. 7 (July 2014): 1482–86.

7   P. Hill, N. Turiano, D. Mrozek, and A. Burrow. "The Value of a Purposeful Life: Sense of Purpose Predicts Greater Income and Net Worth," *Journal of Research in Personality* 65 (December 2016): 38–42.

8   Carol Ryff, and Robert Krueger, *The Oxford Handbook of Integrative Study* (Oxford, England: Oxford Library of Psychology, 2004).

Today, Ed sees people differently than he did ten years ago. Instead of viewing those he deals with as criminals, nuisances, and problems for society, he wants to help them. For example, instead of finding a way to jail homeless people, as he would have in the past, Ed started a program to count and interview the homeless in order to obtain funding to build homeless shelters. He's changing their lives.

Because Ed's deacon salary doesn't come close to replacing his former income, he found a well-paying job working as a bodyguard for an affluent family. He travels the world and protects them using his law enforcement senses and skills. He has resolved his inner conflict, he's helping others, and he's living a life of significance.

Michael Zanger also discovered his life's purpose. Michael realized much earlier than most that the vast majority of people have work they don't enjoy and that most of the work he did was so that he had the financial means to support his love of the outdoors. The time and energy he devoted to work was not fulfilling.

In his thirties, Michael found himself at an "improbable crossroads." He became a single parent with two kids. At that time, he realized that he came home every day mentally and physically exhausted from work and he didn't have any energy left for his family. Michael decided to make his living doing something he loved. In 1979, Shasta Mountain Guides was born. It went on to become one of the most respected guide companies in the world, serving clients from over 130 countries.

For Michael, it was a delight doing what he enjoyed and an unexpected pleasure helping people accomplish what they thought they couldn't. Climbing mountains is no easy feat. Michael has a file cabinet filled with letters from clients telling him how he has made a difference in their lives.

In discovering their purposes, Ed and Michael made changes that drastically improved their lives and the lives of others. They're happier, more fulfilled, and positively impacting the world around them.

But what if you don't know what your purpose is?

In this chapter, we'll focus on gathering the information that will enable you to identify your purpose in life. In the chapters that follow, we'll interpret your answers.

It's not difficult to find your purpose if you know how, and you WILL find it.

Find Your Purpose in Your Past[9]

Although you can answer the following questions on your own, it's best to work with a trusted helper who's curious and a good listener. It can be a friend, a coworker, a therapist, a distant family member, or one of our Certified Guides at *www.truewealthguide.net*. This person should be someone who's never heard your life's stories, who you feel comfortable enough with to share the details of your life, and who will be willing to ask you to dig deep into the details of your stories. For example, it doesn't help to know that you went on vacation to South Carolina. It does help to learn what happened on the trip, how you felt throughout it, and how the events you experienced impacted

---

9   Some questions were adapted with permission from the *Why Discovery Course* by Simon Sinek, Inc.

you. Avoid relying on a very close friend, a spouse, a parent, or a sibling, because they've experienced some of the same things and already have their own perspective regarding what happened.

Now that you've identified your helper, ask him or her to read the Helper Instructions in appendix 1 before proceeding.

When answering the following questions, be sure to:

1. Take your time and focus on events from your own memory and not what others have told you has happened.

2. Where possible, use a story (or stories) from your life to clarify your response. For example, instead of saying your brother was mean, tell the story about the time your brother cut off your cherished doll's hair.

3. Include as much detail as possible. In the doll story, for example: What did the doll look like? Did she or he have a name? How old were you? How old was your brother? Where was the doll when your brother cut off her hair? What did he do with the hair? What did he say to you? How did you react? Etc.

4. Note how each experience made you feel and how it impacted your life.

5. Skip a question if it does not apply to you.

6. If, in response to a question, you remember a story that is painful, consider that it may be important. Not all stories are positive, but they can provide important pieces of you.

Early Childhood Questions

1. What were your relationships like with your mother, father, and siblings, if you had any?

2. What have you learned from each that is part of who you are today?

3. Which stories or events that included your immediate family members impacted who you are today?

4. Was there a specific holiday or tradition that you enjoyed with your family?

5. What about that event did you love?

6. What was special or unique about it?

7. What about your family makes you feel grateful?

8. What about your family do you wish wasn't a part of your life?

9. Which parts of your childhood were happiest?

10. What effect does that childhood happiness have on you now?

11. Who from outside your family played a major role in your life? For example, it could be a grandparent or a close family friend.

12. What did you learn from him or her that you still retain?

13. Which positive yet significant events changed your life's course?

14. How did these events alter the perspective that you have today?

15. Which traumatic events, if any, changed your life's course?

16. How did these events alter the perspective that you have today?

17. How would your family describe you?

18. How did you fit into your family? For example: Did you get along with everyone? Were you an outcast? Were you the youngest and treated like a baby? Were you expected to be the responsible one?

19. How did the other family members fit into your family?

School Years Questions

1. Did you fit into a certain clique? If so, did you actually fit in or just want to fit in?

2. If you were in a clique, would you have preferred to be in another group?

3. What did your parents think of your friends?

4. Who was your best friend, what was he or she like, and what did you do with him or her?

5. Did you ever talk about dreaming of bigger things beyond the scope of your life, such as becoming an astronaut or solving world hunger?

6. How were your grades?

7. Which subjects were your favorites? Why?

8. Which teachers were your favorites? Why?

9. What profoundly affected you either inside or outside the classroom? For example, I had a quirky and nerdy history teacher in my junior year of high school who wasn't particularly good at teaching—at least, that was my opinion of him. One day, his wife came into the classroom. She looked like a supermodel. A girl raised her hand and boldly asked, "How did you get her?" The teacher replied without hesitation, "I asked." Impressed by how easy and simple that seemed, the next day I asked the most beautiful girl in school to go

with me to a concert, and she did. That, of course, prompted classmates to ask me, "How did you get her?" The impact my history teacher had on me is something I still carry—asking makes a big difference. Asking has led to some amazing things in my life. I've met presidents and rock stars, and married the love of my life. All because I asked.

10. How did your family impact your life during your school years, either positively or negatively?

11. Who outside your immediate family played a significant role in your life during your school years and how?

12. What did you learn from them that you carry with you today?

Teen Years Questions

1. During high school, did your personality change and how?

2. Were you popular or unpopular?

3. Did your teachers like you?

4. Which group of people made you feel most comfortable?

5. What was it about them that made you want to be included in the group?

6. What did your friends like most about you?

7. Did you stand out in any way?

8. How did your teachers or coaches influence who you are today?

9. Was high school easy for you or did you have to try hard to do well?

10. If you had to try hard, did you?

11. How does your high school educational experience impact who you are today?

12. What was the best part about high school?

13. What was the worst part of high school? Why?

14. What was your favorite subject? Why?

15. If you could change one thing about your high school experience, what would it be and why would you want to change it?

16. In both social and academic settings, did you like to work alone or with others? Why?

17. What did you do when you weren't in school?

18. What did you enjoy about those activities?

19. Did you feel more yourself at school or at home?

20. What hobbies did you have and what did you love about them?

21. Do you have those same hobbies today?

22. Which important high school experiences haven't I asked you about, if any?

23. What have you learned from those experiences?

24. What about those experiences are still a part of you today?

Life after High School Questions

1. After high school, did you attend college or trade school, go to work, or start a business?

2. Why did you choose that path?

3. What do you like most about your decision regarding which path to choose?

4. Was it a good decision?

If You Attended College Questions

1. Why did you choose the school you attended?

2. Was it a good choice?

3. If you transferred to another college or university, was that a good choice?

4. Did your college provide you with what you had hoped to get out of it?

5. Did you enjoy college?

6. Describe a professor who has had an impact on you.

7. What was your favorite course?

8. How was that course the perfect fit for you?

9. How did you choose your major?

10. Was your major in an area that interested you, or was it something somebody else wanted you to pursue?

11. Was your major a good choice, or would you have preferred to choose another major?

12. If you could attend college over again, what would you do differently?

13. In college, were you more or less social than in high school, and how did this improve your life or make it worse?

14. If you met someone special in college, what was it about him or her that attracted you, and is that quality still with you today?

15. Did your good friends or those you dated have anything in common?

16. Do you still have relationships with anyone from college?

17. Are you surprised that some friendships didn't last?

18. What changed that ended those friendships?

19. Describe a story about a friend that you no longer have.

20. Were you a leader in any organized clubs or groups?

21. Which aspects of your job as a leader were you good at?

22. Which aspects needed improvement?

23. What is the most valuable lesson or experience from college that has benefited who you are today?

Work Life Questions

1. How did you get your first job? For example, were you referred by a friend? Did you get it some other way? Also, was this job the first one you were offered?

2. What did you like about that job?

3. What did you dislike?

4. Which employees had a positive impact on you?

5. Which employees had a negative impact on you?

6. How did someone at work inspire you?

7. Why did you leave that job?

8. Other than money or benefits, why did you seek your next job?

9. Repeat questions 1 through 6 for each job you have held.

10. Do the best parts of each of these jobs have something in common? If so, what?

11. In each of these positions, which bosses enabled you to thrive and be your most productive? Why?

12. Of all your jobs, which two did you enjoy the most, and what did they have in common? For example, the type of people who worked there, the type of work, etc.

13. What experiences at those two jobs helped you to thrive?

14. What was the worst job you've had, and what made it so difficult?

15. If there were a perfect job, how would you describe it?

16. If you've ever had a job that felt like a calling, what was it and why did it feel like a calling?

17. If you didn't have to work, what would you do, or if you've already stopped working, what do you do instead?

18. Other than money and benefits, what do you find rewarding about your work?

19. Would you consider yourself successful or unsuccessful, and why?

20. Do you work better by yourself or with a team?

21. What time of day and where do you work best?

If You've Started Your Own Business Questions

1. Why did you start your own business?

2. Why did you start that particular kind of business?

3. What makes your business unique?

4. What makes you the best person to run this business?

5. How do you naturally thrive in that role?

6. Was there ever a time when you would have preferred to be doing a different type of work?

7. Who did you hire that turned out to be a fantastic worker? Why?

8. What have you learned from them?

9. Would your most loyal employees turn down an opportunity to work at another company for more money, and why?

10. Why do you and your employees love working for your company?

11. Do you have a business partner, and why?

12. How has your business partner improved the business?

13. How has your business partner made you a better person?

14. Do you still feel that having a business partner was the best choice for you and your business?

15. Are you still excited about your business, and why?

16. If you are no longer excited about your business, have you changed or has the business changed?

Spouse or Significant Other Questions

1. What drew you to your spouse or significant other?

2. How would he or she describe you?

3. What aspects of your spouse or your significant other's personality keep you interested in them and keep the relationship alive?

4. What aspects of your personality keep the relationship alive?

5. Why are you grateful for your spouse or significant other?

6. What are the best elements of your relationship?

7. What one thing do you really love about your relationship?

What You Do When You're Not Working Questions

1. What hobbies do you have, and what do you love about them?

2. What's your favorite movie or book, and why?

3. If you participate in any organizations outside of work, what are they and why do you participate in them?

4. Is there something you've always wanted to accomplish but haven't? What is it and why have you not accomplished it?

5. In thinking about the people whom you spend time with outside of work, what draws you to them?

6. Have any of these people made a significant impact on who you are?

7. What three to five things do you enjoy in your free time, not including your hobbies, and why do you enjoy them?

8. How do you manage your free time? Do you have a routine, or do you do what you feel like at any given time? For example, I'm a list guy even when on vacation. I get specific things done each day. That's how I feel comfortable, and it makes my life less stressful if I know what I need to do and check things off on a list rather than trying to remember things or making last-minute decisions about what I need to do.

Congratulations, you've dug deep into your life and identified the events, stories, and aspects that make you...you. At this time, you no longer need your helper. But you will need him or her again when you reach chapter 4, where I'll show you how to use the information you obtained together to discover your purpose.

But first, let's look at how your purpose unlocks your potential.

CHAPTER 3

U: Unlock Your Potential

WHAT IS POTENTIAL? ACCORDING TO THE MERRIAM WEBSTER COLLEGIATE DICTIONARY,[10] IT'S "HAVING or showing the capacity to become or develop into something in the future."

I think it's the power to fulfill your greatest dreams. But it's impossible to achieve your potential without knowing your purpose. Purpose enables you to know where you're going; it gives you direction. It's that simple.

As you think about finding your purpose, there are two things to keep in mind. The first is that, ultimately, your purpose in life is not about you; it's about how you impact others and make the world a better place. The second is that no one else can find your purpose for you.

Before we get started, let me tell you about a story I read recently in the *Los Angeles Times*[11] that showed how your purpose is not about you. Former college football player James Holland was a Texas Ranger, a detective who dealt with the state's most serious crimes. James quickly found his purpose—getting serial killers to confirm and confess their crimes, one of whom admitted killing ninety-three women. He succeeded where many others failed because he realized the job was not about him and his success. It was about helping the victims' family members heal as a result of learning what happened to their loved ones. Holland states it's that purpose that drives him. He

---

10   Merriam Webster Collegiate Dictionary, 11th ed., 2003.

11   Del Quintin Weber, "A Texas Ranger Got a Prolific Serial Killer to Talk," *Los Angeles Times*, September 26, 2019.

feels an enormous responsibility to the families of the victims and has learned from experience and training how to communicate with psychopaths.

James Holland fulfilled his potential through his purpose.

Now it's time for you to find yours.

In knowing your purpose, you reveal your authentic self, you trust yourself, and others trust you. You start to attract people and things that support your purpose, often without trying. With a clearly articulated purpose, you have the capacity to develop your purpose into something great in the future—your potential.

Let me explain the link between purpose and potential.

Knowing Your Purpose Impacts Your Life

The desire to create a better life and a better world gives you enormous power. But desire alone is not enough. You must have purpose too. Purpose drives your desire.

Without purpose, things become pretty ordinary, routine, and aimless. For example, one of the greatest joys of a parent or grandparent is being able to relive seeing the world for the first time—enjoying the excitement when your child or grandchild gets his first puppy or sees his first snowfall. You feel that excitement all over again as if you too are experiencing those things with them for the first time.

The first time you experience something, it's extraordinary and remarkable. But as you experience the same thing over and over, you gradually lose enthusiasm. What once was exciting becomes routine and without purpose; it becomes commonplace or ordinary. For example, shoveling snow might be exciting the first time you do it, but after you shovel snow thirty times, it's not an exciting experience—it's a chore.

When excitement and purpose are lost (or when purpose is never discovered to begin with), life becomes ordinary and routine. There's no path forward, only aimless wandering.

But when you discover your purpose, aimless wandering becomes intentional movement. Choices become obvious. The questions that you can ask yourself about furthering and supporting your purpose become apparent. When you know your purpose, you know where you're going. Purpose gives you direction and unlocks your potential, which ultimately enables you to impact others.

Knowing Your Purpose Can Impact Others

Millard Fuller, the founder of Habitat for Humanity, had one goal early in life—to get rich. He went from sharecropper to direct mail millionaire before the age of thirty, but his preoccupation with money took a toll on his personal life. When his long absences and lack of attention became intolerable, his wife Linda left with their two children and mulled over whether or not to get a divorce.

Fuller was devastated and became another example of the miserable rich. But to his credit, he reevaluated his values and redefined his purpose, deciding on a life of living simply and a "theology of enough."

To prove to Linda that she was more important to him than money, he sold his business and his possessions and gave the money to charity. Millard and his family reunited, focusing on the values they deemed most important, and a bigger shared purpose came into view—to teach basic construction skills to families who couldn't afford homes. These skills would enable the families to build homes and, together, to build a community. After building several thousand homes in Zaire, Africa, with volunteer help and interest-free loans, Millard and Linda created a non-profit entity to support their purpose.

Habitat for Humanity was born in 1976 and has become the largest non-profit builder in the world. To date, Habitat has built over 800,000 homes in nearly a hundred countries, providing shelter and building community for more than four million people.

That's the power of purpose.

Like Fuller, once you discover your true purpose, your journey will become exciting. You'll follow a vision that inspires you. Decisions will become obvious. Passion will give you the energy you need to work through difficulties. It will become clear what is and isn't important. And you'll begin to attract like-minded people. Apple founders Steve Jobs and Steve Wozniak were introduced by a mutual friend who knew that they both liked electronics and that they both wanted to build a computer. Beatles band member John Lennon met Paul McCartney at a musical event, each impressing the other with his talent.

Knowing my purpose has made my journey exciting again and inspires me each day. I'm happier and full of passion. It's like the juice has turned back on. Instead of working toward my retirement, I'm working on doing more for my clients and for my family. Knowing my purpose drives me to work hard each day to further my purpose. Nothing about developing The GUIDE Process or writing this book is boring or routine. I'm squeezing the time to work on it into what was already a full life, and I'm doing it by choice because I know helping others to create their ideal life and to find True Wealth will impact the world.

Now that you know how your purpose unlocks your potential, it's time to identify patterns and motifs in your stories, which will enable you to find your purpose.

CHAPTER 4

I: Identify Patterns and Motifs

I WAS SEVEN YEARS OLD WHEN MY FAMILY MOVED FROM CALIFORNIA TO OKLAHOMA. MY GRANDPARENTS, whom we had spent a lot of time with, met us on the roadside somewhere near Bakersfield, California, for a very tearful goodbye. I vividly remember looking at my grandparents out of the rear car window as we drove away and until they were out of sight. They were sobbing the entire time. I wasn't crying, however, because I didn't understand what they were feeling.

As I look back on that day, I feel a deep sense of sadness that almost brings tears to my eyes because I now understand why they were so upset. Instead of spending summers and holidays with them, we would be able to see them only twice over the next eleven years.

As we drove, the trip became a fabulous adventure. We'd never been on a vacation, so everything we saw and did was exciting and new. First, we went to Las Vegas and played the slot machines at Caesar's Palace. Next, we saw the Grand Canyon and Hoover Dam. Then we made our way down to the Meteor Crater in Arizona, followed by a drive to see the Alamo in San Antonio, Texas. I loved going to these new places, learning new things, and discovering the history associated with them. And, I loved Oklahoma. Looking back, those were the best years for my family because we felt safe and at home there.

Over the years, our family moved often, and I attended thirteen schools by the time I finished my education. Eventually, we moved back to California and I was able to spend a lot of time with my grandparents again.

What's important about this story is that family and stability are key factors in my life. For the past forty years, I've lived with my wife in the same town. My kids and grandkids live in the same town until they go off to college, and we see each other almost every day.

What stays with me from this story is that I have a peacefulness and optimism about the future. And because the move to Oklahoma was fantastic, exploring new places, ideas, and things are a big piece of my identity. I'm also able to find compassion for others, such as the compassion I now feel for my grandparents, understanding how they must have felt on the day of our move. These themes are repeated in my stories.

Themes in Your Life's Stories

In order to figure out your purpose, you must identify patterns and motifs in your life, the keys that are hidden in the stories from your past. With your helper, you're going to dig deeper into the stories to understand the impact they have had on your life. The website *www.truewealthguide. net* includes a digital notebook with helpful suggestions.

Work separately and in different spaces so you're not tempted to compare notes at this time. The purpose is to obtain differing perspectives. Each of you will look for connecting threads between the stories—themes, conversations, and recurring practices (things you do repeatedly)—and write them down. Those are your DNA. "D" stands for your defining moments, "N" stands for your natural contributions, and "A" stands for how you are appreciated by others. When most people do this, the themes will jump off the page. You may discover ten to twenty. For example, when I was young, my parents purchased the *World Book Encyclopedia*. The books were white with blue bands on the spine. With a frenzy, I read from "A" to "Z," cover to cover, because I love to learn and explore new ideas. That passion has shown up time and time again throughout my life, and I still have it today, for which I am grateful. A passion for learning and exploring has enabled me to learn new things, investigate new businesses and opportunities, and encourage others to try new things, such as convincing more than one hundred people who hadn't planned to go bungee jumping to bungee jump in New Zealand. Most of them thanked me.

Now, decide which four to six themes you feel are most important, most impactful, and are truly you—themes you know you want to pursue—and rank them in order of importance. Your helper should do the same with the themes he discovered. It's important for your helper to rank the themes because he may notice something that you didn't. For example, my helper told me that what I really liked doing was bettering others' lives, which I didn't even notice was a theme. However, it fit pretty nicely with my life, made sense, and worked well with themes of potential, optimism, and the others that I had identified in my stories.

Once both you and your helper have compiled your theme lists (if you can't find any themes, don't worry; I'll address that later), compare notes to make sure you've gotten their perspective and they've gotten yours. Be sure to tell your helper how you feel about each of the themes. It's the feeling you're going after. The actual words are not as important as their meaning. You can change the words later, but the feeling has to be right. If you have the right feeling, you'll know it. For example, a theme for me was helping others. But it was the feeling that came with that theme—empowering—and not the words "helping others" that was important. The words change as you work with them and put them into practice, but the meaning and the associated feeling remain the same.

Phone a Friend

Consult three or four friends individually—either in person or via telephone—and tell them you are attempting to find your purpose and that he or she can help. Then ask: Why are you friends with me?

Your friend might say he doesn't know why he's friends with you, or give a generic answer like "you're funny," but be patient and wait for him to give you a reason. If, after a while, he still doesn't know, ask him to tell you a story about something you've done together and how the events in the story made him feel. For example, a good friend said, after we discussed something we'd done together, "I feel really comfortable doing things that I wouldn't ordinarily do [when I do them] with you." My next question was: "What happens as a result?" to which she replied, "I open up as a person. I see things from a different perspective, and I feel very safe trying new things or things out of the ordinary."

But I didn't stop there. I dug deeper, trying to discover the root of why she was friends with me. I asked, "So I make you feel safe enough to try things you wouldn't ordinarily do?" When she replied yes, I asked, "And when you do that, how do you feel?" She responded that she's learned about different places and cultures. "I feel like I can do things I never thought possible."

The important part to remember about this exercise is to keep asking questions until you are satisfied you know what aspects of your personality make your friend feel better about himself and/or his life as a result of being friends with you. What do you give to him that he otherwise might not have?

Once you go through this process with three or four friends, a pattern should emerge. Your friends will state similar reasons for wanting to be friends with you. These are your themes. For example, I make my friends feel comfortable and more willing to try new things.

What Do You Like?

Here's an example of how asking a few simple questions enabled a taxi driver to discover the themes in his life and how they led to discovering his purpose.

A businessman flew into Chicago and took a taxi from the airport to his hotel. When the businessman tried to engage the taxi driver in conversation, the driver ignored him; the driver didn't seem happy. So, the businessman wanted to find a way to improve the taxi driver's mood. He asked, "What do you love about your job?"

The taxi driver replied, "Nothing. I hate every bit of this job. It sucks. I'd quit doing it if I didn't have bills to pay."

That didn't discourage the businessman. He asked, "Is there any part of your day that you do love?"

The taxi driver said, "Yeah, I coach a kids soccer team when I get off work. I can't wait to get off work so I can coach the kids." He paused then said, "I know what you're getting at— you're looking for the happy parts of my life. But really this just sucks."

The businessman asked, "Is there any part of your job or any group of people that you enjoy?"

"Yeah," the taxi driver said. "I like older women. I like to take care of them. They need more help with their luggage. And I like taking them to their place and making sure they're safe. And I feel really good about it."

The taxi driver feels fulfilled when he works with older women even though he hates his job. He now is working to find or create a job doing only what he enjoys—working with older women. For example, using the skills he acquired as a taxi driver, he could drive for a business that transports elderly women to and from doctor's and other appointments.

Now ask yourself:

1. What do you like doing that you're really good at?

2. Is there any part of what you do that you love doing, and why?

3. If not, is there any part of your day that you love, and why?

4. Is there a group of people you particularly enjoy working with? If so, what about working with them makes you feel good?

5. How do these people feel about working with you?

Completing this section can help define not only what you enjoy doing, but also what you're good at. It's the final piece of the puzzle.

Choosing Motifs

Now that you have gathered the information you need:

1. Work with your helper and examine what you discovered in Themes in Your Life's Stories, What Do You Like?, and Phone a Friend.

2. Decide together which stories or events have transformed your life and made you who you are today. Most likely, they will grab your attention immediately.

3. Determine the motifs in those stories or events, the recurring ideas or themes that you discovered.

4. Separate from your helper, rank your motifs in order of importance to you. Your helper should do the same.

5. Discuss your top four to six motifs with your helper (he should discuss his top four to six motifs with you as well) and together decide which two are the most important. The first should show what you do that helps others (action). The second should demonstrate the impact your contribution has on others (result).

Now that you know the important themes and motifs in your life, it's time to discover your purpose and develop your purpose statement.

CHAPTER 5

D: Develop Your Purpose Statement

IN THIS CHAPTER YOU WILL LEARN THE IMPORTANCE OF A PURPOSE STATEMENT AND HOW TO CRAFT YOURS.

A purpose statement helps you in every area of your life. When you can articulate your purpose clearly, you can share it with others; and when you can share it with others, the excitement regarding your purpose spreads. You'll see this when you meet someone for the first time—a stranger on an airplane or someone at a cocktail party—and tell them your purpose. They'll take an interest, get excited about your purpose, and share that excitement with others.

A Purpose Statement Helps Guide Your Decision Making

When you don't have a purpose statement, it's like driving your car on a vacation without a destination in mind. You're wandering randomly, wondering if you should go left or right, not knowing where you're going or how you'll get there. When you have a purpose statement, it's like using a driving app. When you know where you want to go, it's a lot easier to make decisions regarding which way to turn.

A Purpose Statement Helps You Focus on What's Important to Do Right Now

Each day we have a number of things that we want to accomplish. For me, one is to work on this book during the weekend, because weekends are when I have the most time to concentrate on it.

But each weekend is filled with other opportunities, particularly when the weather is nice and the outside's calling me. Without my purpose statement in mind, I might sleep in and then join my family outside for fun activities. However, because I know my purpose and my purpose statement, and because writing this book will enable me to fulfill that purpose, I wake up early and write for several hours while everyone else is sleeping. This enables me to move toward my purpose and to have fun with my family.

A Purpose Statement Helps You in Every Area of Your Life

Having a purpose statement enables you to know where you're going and what you want to accomplish. It enables you to know what steps you need to take to get there. The desire to do something big and challenging will inspire you to high levels of creativity. Having a purpose statement will give you extra energy and make you feel more confident and happier. Knowing the why behind your dream will maximize your chance of achieving it. It will positively impact your health and your relationships with others. It will impact every area of your life. According to Oprah Winfrey, "There is no greater gift than to honor your life's calling."

Millard Fuller Test

Remember Millard Fuller, the founder of Habitat for Humanity? His original purpose was to get rich; however, his purpose didn't match his values, so he didn't feel fulfilled. Once he reevaluated what was important in his life and aligned his life with his values, he found his true purpose, and True Wealth.

Values define who you are. They are aspects of your personality that drive your actions. When your values align with how you conduct your life, you feel fulfilled and satisfied. When your values don't align with how you conduct your life, you feel like something's missing, like you should be doing something else with your life, but you often don't know what, or even what's wrong. If you want to feel fulfilled, your values and your purpose must align.

Let's start by aligning your values with the themes and motifs you gathered from your stories to ensure you impact others in a way that supports your values.

Circle as many or as few of the values listed in the following categories that define you.

Feelings: acceptance, comfort, compassion, contentment, empathy, grace, gratitude, happiness, hope, inspire, joy, kindness, love, optimism, passion, peace, poise, respect, reverence, satisfaction, serenity, thankfulness, tranquility, and welcoming.

Achievement: accomplishment, capable, challenge, competence, credibility, determination, development, drive, effectiveness, empower, endurance, excellence, growth, hard work, improvement, influence, intensity, leadership, mastery, motivation, performance, persistence, potential, power, productivity, professionalism, recognition, results, risk, significance, skill, success, talent, and intelligence.

Brilliance: clever, common sense, decisiveness, foresight, genius, insightfulness, knowledge, learning, logic, openness, realistic, reason, reflective, smart, thoughtful, understanding, vision, and wisdom.

Strength: ambition, assertiveness, boldness, confidence, dedication, discipline, fortitude, persistence, power, restraint, rigor, self-reliance, temperance, toughness, vigor, and will.

Freedom: independence, individuality, and liberty.

Courage: bravery, conviction, fearless, valor.

Creativity: creation, curiosity, discovery, exploration, expressive, imagination, innovation, inquisitive, intuitive, openness, originality, uniqueness, wonder.

Enjoyment: amusement, enthusiasm, experience, fun, playfulness, recreation, spontaneity, surprise.

Order: accuracy, careful, certainty, cleanliness, consistency, control, decisive, economy, justice, lawful, moderation, organization, security, stability, structure, thorough, and timeliness.

Health: energy and vitality.

Presence: alertness, attentive, awareness, beauty, calm, clear, concentration, focus, silence, simplicity, and solitude.

Spirituality: adaptability, altruism, balance, charity, communication, community, connection, conscientiousness, contribution, cooperation, courtesy, devotion, equality, ethics, fairness, family, fidelity, friendship, generosity, giving, goodness, harmony, humility, loyalty, maturity, meaning, selflessness, sensitivity, service, sharing, spirit, stewardship, support, sustainability, teamwork, tolerance, and unity.

Now that you've circled the values that define you, highlight those that are most important to you and that you want to pursue. These are your true values.[12]

---

12   Adapted from Tchiki Davis, "39 Core Values—and How to Live by Them," *Psychology Today*, July 12, 2018 (Sussex Publishers, LLC), *https://www.psychologytoday.com/us/blog/click-here-happiness/201807/39-core-values-and-how-live-them.*

Using Your Themes and Values to Discover Your Purpose

Now that you know your themes (from chapter 4) and values, it's time to discover your purpose.

Compare the themes in your stories to your most important values. Do the themes and how they make you feel match your values? For example, some of my values were optimism, potential, and empowerment. Those values felt the same to me as the themes that emerged from my stories where I was helping people.

If your themes don't match your values, refocus on your most important values—similar to Millard Fuller when he discovered he no longer valued being rich but valued helping others —and see how the values differ from the themes in your stories. Thinking about your stories more deeply, look at each story with a new perspective, asking yourself: In what ways did the story impact me that I hadn't noticed before now? Can I draw anything else from the lessons I learned from the events in the story? If you fail to discover something new, move on to other stories, ones that didn't make it onto your most important list but are impactful and support your values. You might think of new stories you hadn't considered previously, which is okay. Discuss the stories with your helper to ensure they support your values.

To determine your purpose, decide which one value of those you identified as your most important is most impactful in your life and to others. That is your purpose. If you can't narrow your list to one value, if several seem equal and important, craft a purpose statement for each, and determine which purpose statement feels most authentic to you.

How to Craft a Purpose Statement

Now that you know your purpose, you need a way to articulate it to others.

With your helper, complete the following four parts of your purpose statement. Detailed examples showing completed purpose statements follow the exercise.

My purpose is to _____ *(action that you take or what you do that benefits others)*

For example: My purpose is to teach; my purpose is to motivate; my purpose is to inspire.

_____ *(who benefits)*

For example, children, firemen, entrepreneurs, or simply everyone.

so that _____ *(what the person who benefits hopes to accomplish or attain)*

and, in doing so, _____ *(the impact on the greater good)*

For example, the greater good could be a football team, people in general, the entire world.

Let's see how Oprah Winfrey would develop her purpose statement.

In an October 21, 2019, issue of *People Magazine*,[13] Oprah Winfrey stated her purpose was to inspire students to be more than they ever thought they would be. She discussed two defining moments that related to her purpose. The first was when she moved from Milwaukee to Nashville, which gave her a different view of the world and helped her develop empathy for people who "were smart and vibrant and hopeful and that got smothered and overwhelmed." The second was when she worked on a television talk show that sensationalized a husband, a wife, and his pregnant mistress. As a result of these experiences, she decided to make an intentional effort to be a good force in people's lives. The constant thread in her life is the positive impact she has on other people's lives and how she feels like she has become more than she ever thought possible. Inspiring people enabled her to do that.

Using the above details, Oprah's purpose statement would be:

My purpose is to inspire my students so they become more than they ever thought they could be and, in doing so, more people would accept their calling.

Remember Simon Sinek and the Golden Circle? In *Start with Why*,[14] he writes, "My purpose is to inspire people to do the things that inspire them so that together we can change the world."

For me, the first draft of my purpose statement was:

My purpose is to help others so that they discover their purpose and, in doing so, unleash the full power of all human potential.

I soon realized that my purpose was flawed because my purpose was only to help others to discover their purpose. But I really wanted to show them a process to find their purpose and unlock their full potential. I rewrote it to state:

*My purpose is to help others to discover their purpose, unlock their potential and, in doing so, **together we** can unleash the full power of all human potential.*

Lastly, if Gandhi had written his purpose statement, it would be:

My purpose is to teach passive resistance to oppressed people so they can overcome injustice and, in doing so, we create more peace and cooperation in the world.

---

13   Mary Green, "The Five Moments That Changed My Life," *People*, October 21, 2019.

14   Simon Sinek, *Start with Why* (New York, NY: Portfolio, 2009).

Now that you've seen a few purpose statements and completed yours, ask your helper if your purpose statement describes you. If he says yes, great. If he says no, talk about what needs to change in the purpose statement and make those changes here.

My purpose is to _____ *(action that you take or*

what you do that benefits others) _____ *(who benefits)*

so that _____ *(what the person who benefits*

hopes to accomplish or attain) and, in doing so, _____

_____ *(the impact on the greater good)*

You now have your one-sentence purpose statement.

As you can see, your purpose statement brings together how your purpose, potential, and ideal life fit together, and how it will impact every area of your life.

Now that you have your purpose statement, you need to know how to use it in the real world.

CHAPTER 6

E: Evaluate and Evolve

YOU MUST EVALUATE AND EVOLVE YOUR PURPOSE STATEMENT AS YOU PUT YOUR PURPOSE INTO ACTION. For example, you might start out by saying that you want to help people in Africa have clean drinking water. But, in order to do that, you must teach them how to purify water.

Your purpose statement would evolve from:

My purpose is to help people in Africa have clean drinking water, so they don't get sick from the water and, in doing so, they can live better, healthier lives.

to:

My purpose is to teach people in Africa to purify water, so they don't get sick from the water and, in doing so, they can live better, healthier lives.

The purpose statement evolved from asking, "What exactly will I do to help people have clean water?" to "How will I do it?"

You also can evolve the purpose statement to narrow or broaden who you want to help. In the above example, you could narrow your statement to include only a specific region in Africa or broaden it to include the entire world. For example, if you narrowed your focus, you purpose statement would evolve to:

My purpose is to teach water purification to people in Zaire, Africa, so they don't get sick from the water and, in doing so, they can live better, healthier lives.

As you seek to revise your statement, refer back to your stories and values. Keep in mind that you don't want to change the meaning of your purpose statement; you just want it to feel more specific and applicable.

Here's another example of how to evaluate and evolve your purpose statement.

Claire wants to help people with anxiety. Her initial purpose statement is:

My purpose is to help people with anxiety cope better with the events in their lives and, in doing so, improve the quality of their lives and the lives of those they interact with.

As Claire starts to talk to people who work with those suffering from anxiety, she evaluates and evolves her purpose statement, narrowing her focus to using equine therapy in order to help those suffering from post-traumatic stress disorder (PTSD). She further evolves her statement by narrowing her focus to helping veterans suffering from PTSD live a less anxious life.

Claire's revised purpose statement is:

My purpose is to use equine therapy to help soldiers suffering from PTSD cope with anxiety and, in doing so, improve the quality of their lives and the lives of those they interact with.

Claire might choose to evolve her statement further by focusing on only male or female soldiers, or only soldiers who fought in the Gulf War. She also might evolve her statement to include wanting to help the soldiers better cope with living outside of a war zone or to help them improve their interactions with their families.

After thinking things through, Claire further revises her purpose statement to:

My purpose is to use equine therapy to help soldiers with PTSD and who are reentering civilian life better cope with living with their families and, in doing so, create a more peaceful and harmonious world for them all.

Test-Driving Your Purpose Statement

Now it's time to test-drive your purpose statement on people you don't know—people you meet on an airplane, at a party, at a fundraiser, etc. Tell them your purpose statement and talk about what's important to you and the experiences that have led you to where you are today. Of course, you let the conversation develop naturally. If I were settling in on a three-hour flight, I wouldn't start the conversation with my seatmate saying, "I'm Mark, my purpose is..." It might look something like this:

"So, where is home for you? And what do you do?"

He might tell you that he's a professor at a university.

"Oh, and what subject do you teach?"

He might say, "Anthropology, and what do you do?"

"I'm a partner at Enso Wealth Management. I specialize in helping clients find their true calling in life and being able to finance it."

"And how do you do that?" he may respond.

"I have a process…"

Mentally note his responses. What conversations result from discussing your purpose statement? I think you will find that many people are excited to hear your story. But keep in mind that people have different interests. Not everyone will want to jump aboard your train. Don't worry. Keep spreading your purpose and you will find others interested, curious, and enthusiastic.

As you talk to people, you'll begin to reevaluate your purpose statement, asking yourself: What am I doing? Why am I doing it? What happens when I do it? How do people benefit as a result of me doing this? What is the impact on the greater good? The answers will clarify your purpose statement. For example, my initial purpose statement was to help others. When I asked myself what I wanted to do to help others, I realized that I wanted to write this book to give others a process for finding their purpose, unlocking their potential, and ultimately achieving True Wealth. As a result of that realization, my purpose statement evolved to:

My purpose is to empower others to discover their purpose and unlock their potential and, in doing so, together we can unleash the full power of all human potential.

Implementing Your Purpose Statement

In order to impact your life and the lives of others, you must implement your purpose statement. Without action, nothing will change, and you'll be back where you started. It's like paying for a gym membership but never going to the gym. You never get any benefit from it. You don't gain muscle, lose weight, feel better, or increase your energy by paying the gym membership. In addition, your bank account is worse off, and that's the only thing that changes. You benefit when you use your membership.

Once you put your purpose statement into action and live your purpose, opportunities are limitless. Your purpose might take you places you hadn't expected, enable you to do things you never considered, or open you up to new ideas. You may find yourself like Millard Fuller, who started the world's largest nonprofit building organization, or like Oprah, who inspired many people to be more than they thought they could be. Or you could be like me and write a book that will empower people to live their purpose.

But in order to implement your purpose statement, you will need to figure out your finances.

PART II

The GUIDE for Finances

PLANNING YOUR FINANCES
TO SUPPORT YOUR IDEAL LIFE

CHAPTER 7

A Purpose-Driven Financial Plan

AT THIS POINT YOU'VE COMPLETED A NUMBER OF EXERCISES AND ANSWERED QUESTIONS TO DEFINE your purpose. It's important that you plan your finances to support it. Without a financial plan, you're likely to hit bumps in the road that you're not prepared for, and it could derail your plan entirely. With a financial plan, your chances of success are greatly enhanced. But you'll need an action plan to accomplish it. To do that, I'll return to the financial planning process and again convert it to The GUIDE Process, this time to finance your ideal life.

1. Step One became   **G**et your financial information together.

2. Step Two became   **U**nderstand what's important.

3. Step Three became   **I**nvest with confidence.

4. Step Four became   **D**evelop your ideal financial plan.

5. Step Five became   **E**valuate and evolve.

Completing these steps will enable you to fulfill your purpose and unlock your potential to make a huge contribution to the world.

Purpose + Financial Plan = True Wealth

A husband and wife in their forties, who had been my clients for at least ten years, had not completed a financial plan. I asked them: "Is there anything you haven't yet accomplished that you really want to get done in your life?" Immediately, they stated they wanted to sail the Mediterranean for a month with their children. They would visit a number of ports that place happiness above material wealth, places they would like to see protected and sustained for future generations. They even talked about where they would get provisions. But I got the feeling they thought it was impossible, that they dreamed about the trip but never thought they could accomplish it.

In looking at the details and the cost of the trip, we figured out how much they needed to save to allow them to take the trip, while still having enough money to retire comfortably. With a plan in place, they realized their goal is attainable. Now, they have an enormous feeling of satisfaction that they're going to accomplish what was once a wild dream.

The wife said, "The financial plan went from esoteric and mundane—here's what you need to do to keep paying for groceries—to a tangible concrete result of all of my hard work. It gives me a plan for an exciting life. My purpose is to inspire others to protect and care for places and cultures that still cherish happiness above material wealth."

Once she knew her purpose, it was a game-changing event. It's what she was born to do. Putting her purpose into action lit up her life and made her feel fulfilled.

Let's look at another example of how having a purpose-driven financial plan enables you to achieve True Wealth and live your ideal life.

Lori-Ann Murphy's family fished a lot when she was growing up, but she had never gone fly-fishing. While attending nursing school in Seattle, Lori-Ann went on a fly-fishing trip on the Deschutes River and landed her first steelhead. That experience started Lori-Ann on an entirely new life path—a path with purpose.

Because Lori-Ann loved fly-fishing, she started spending more time fly-fishing while she was in nursing school. After she graduated, she accepted a job in Wyoming—except she never got there. On the way, she stopped for a little river time in Driggs, Idaho. She loved Driggs, so instead of continuing to Wyoming, she found a nursing position in the local hospital. That granted Lori-Ann a new life that included regular fly-fishing.

With her natural ability and with practice, she perfected the art of fly-fishing, knowing how to lay the fly over the water where the fish would take it. Soon, she met the guy who would become her husband. He was a fishing guide, and he encouraged her to use her expert fly-fishing skills to become a guide as well.

One day, Lori-Ann attended the Orvis Rendezvous in Montana, a trade show for fishing guides, and ended up fishing with Leigh Perkins, who owns The Orvis Company. As a result of that fateful meeting, Lori-Ann became the first woman guide whom Orvis endorsed.

In 1994, she started Reel Women Fly Fishing Adventures and became the first company to offer women-only fly-fishing trips all over the world. Her purpose is to ignite women who have a passion for fly-fishing and to provide adventures to realize their limitless potential.

Lori-Ann has been featured on ESPN and was the fly-fishing technical advisor for the movie *A River Wild*, with Meryl Streep. My wife and I were lucky enough to have Lori-Ann as our guide while on a trip to Jackson Hole, Wyoming. While we fished, we talked business, planning, and purpose. Lori-Ann's passion for fishing led to a life that she loves. Once she knew her purpose, the money followed. It enabled her to quit nursing and pursing her fly-fishing passion.

Fly-fishing is Lori-Ann's life. She's moved to Ambergris Caye, Belize, for nine months of the year, where she provides guided fly-fishing experiences. The rest of the year she lives in the Pacific Northwest and spends her time as a fly-fishing guide. Lori-Ann is so glad she took that first fly-fishing trip on the Driggs river, because today she is living her dream and not worrying about how to finance it.

Realizing Your Purpose Statement

If you're like most people who want to make a change in your life, money's the hang-up. In order to support your ideal life, you must create income or investments. Retiring, taking vacations, or accepting a lower-paying job costs money. But remember, money shouldn't be the guiding choice of your decision. You want to make the money fit the life, not the life fit the money. Figuring out how much money you make and trying to make your life fit inside of that boundary limits your choices and will leave you unfulfilled.

You can't live the life you want without figuring out the finances—you still have bills to pay. Before you can quit your job, you need to put together a plan that will allow you to make a transition without going broke in the process.

Planning will provide you with an analysis of your current situation and a roadmap to pursue your ideal life experience. Without planning, it's highly unlikely that you're going to successfully change careers or evolve what you currently do.

If you figure out what's important, it will enable you to move from the life you have now to living your ideal life. The questions and exercises in the chapters that follow help you do just that.

CHAPTER 8

G: Getting Your Current Financial Information Together

THIS PART OF THE BOOK BEGINS BY FOCUSING ON GATHERING THE RELEVANT FINANCIAL INFORMATION that will enable you to create your ideal life and make your purpose statement a reality in the practical world.

To figure out how to finance your ideal life, you first must determine your current income and expenses by completing the Simple Cash Flow Analysis Form below. If you are unable to answer a question, such as total household expenses, complete the Data Gathering Form in appendix 2, which breaks down how to calculate expenses and income in more detail. Then return here and use the information you obtained from completing the Data Gathering Form to complete the Simple Cash Flow Analysis Form.

The Simple Cash Flow Analysis Form has three columns. The first is for your finances; the second is for your husband, wife, or partner's finances, if applicable; and the third is for your combined income and expenses.

To complete the Simple Cash Flow Analysis Form:

1. Monthly Gross Income Section

    a. List your W2 income, which is your monthly gross income, in the first column.

    b. List additional income such as business, Social Security, rental, investment, alimony, royalties, gifts, etc., below your W2 income where indicated.

    c.   Total your income from all sources and write the amount where it says "total."

    d.   Repeat the above for your spouse, significant other, or partner's Monthly Gross Income, putting those numbers in the second column as indicated.

    e.   Add your and your partners income in the total income space (I).

2.   Monthly Deductions Section

    a.   List federal, state, and Social Security taxes.

    b.   List retirement plan and college savings contributions.

    c.   Write your household spending here (refer to your Data Gathering Form, if necessary).

    d.   Include your medical expenses and travel costs in the respective spaces.

    e.   Add your total deductions together and write the amount in the "total deductions space."

    f.   Repeat the above for your spouse, significant other, or partner's monthly deductions, putting those numbers in the second column as indicated.

    g.   Add your and your partners deductions in the total deductions space (D).

3.   Debt Section

    a.   List the balance owed on your home, automobiles, credit cards, and other debts, along with the monthly payment amount and expected payoff date on their respective lines.

    b.   Total balances owed and write the amount where it states "total" at the bottom of that column.

    c.   Total the monthly payments and list them in the total payments space (P).

4.   In the third column add the totals of debt payments and deductions and enter that number in space (S).

5.   (I) minus (S) = Cash Flow.

Knowing your actual cash flow will allow you to make realistic projections for financing your ideal life. Without knowing your cash flow, which most people don't, you will make projections that are far from accurate. This happens because most people don't have a clear-cut view of what they really spend. For example, if someone tells me they have a positive cash flow of $3,000 a month, I'll ask them, "Well, where do you keep those savings? Based upon what you're telling me, you should be saving $36,000 a year. If it's a husband and wife, they usually look at each other wondering what's going on, because they're actually spending more than they think.

	You	Partner	Combined
Income			
W-2			
Business			
Social Security			
Rental			
Pension			
Investment			
Other			
Total Income (I)			$ _____
Deductions			
Tax			
Retirement Contributions			
Medical			
Household			
Travel			
Other			
Total Deductions (D)			$ _____
Debt Payments (P)			$ _____
D + P = S			$ _____
Cash Flow (I − S)			$ _____

On the next page is an example of a Simple Cash Flow statement for a hypothetical fifty-five-year-old. We have converted from monthly to annual income and expense.

Our fifty-five-year-old planner earns $100,000 a year at her job. She has no other sources of income, pays $20,000 in taxes, and saves $15,000 for retirement. In addition to her $50,000 household expenses, she has a small medical expense of $3,000 per year (because she receives an insurance benefit from her employer), and a small travel budget. The only debt payment she has is her $833.33 per month mortgage ($10,000 per year). Her total income is $100,000 and her total spending is $100,000, resulting in zero cash flow.

Cash Flow—Age 55

	You	Partner	Combined
Income			
W-2	100,000		
Business			
Social Security			
Rental			
Pension			
Investment			
Other			
Total Income (I)	100,000		**$ 100,000**
Deductions			
Tax	20,000		
Retirement Contributions	15,000		
Medical	3,000		
Household	50,000		
Travel	2,000		
Other			
Total Deductions (D)			**$ 90,000**
Debt Payments (P)			**$ 10,000**
D + P = S			**$ 100,000**
Cash Flow (I − S)		100,000 − 100,000	**$ 0**

In example #2 on the opposite page, our planner is projecting her cash flow with an intent to retire at age sixty. She would have no income from work, and her only source of income would be her retirement savings. Because her income would be lower, her taxes would be as well ($10,000). Her medical expenses would increase from $3,000 to $8,000 because she would no longer be covered under her employer's plan. Her household expenses would remain the same, but her retirement contributions would have ceased. Her total projected income of $32,000 would come from investment assets (her retirement savings). Her total spending would be $80,000, resulting in a negative $48,000 cash flow. She doesn't have enough income to support her expenses.

Cash Flow—Age 60

	You	Partner	Combined
Income			
W-2			
Business			
Social Security			
Rental			
Pension			
Investment	32,000		
Other			
Total Income (I)	32,000		**$ 32,000**
Deductions			
Tax	10,000		
Retirement Contributions	0		
Medical	8,000		
Household	50,000		
Travel	2,000		
Other			
Total Deductions (D)			**$ 70,000**
Debt Payments (P)			**$ 10,000**
D + P = S			**$ 80,000**
Cash Flow (I − S)		32,000 − 80,000	**-$ 48,000**

She has options! She could choose to downsize her house, reduce her spending, increase her income and savings during that period, or delay her retirement.

In example #3 on p.58, she elects to retire at age sixty-five. She would have no income from work but would receive $30,000 from Social Security. Her taxes would decline, and medical expenses would decrease to $3,000 because she would be eligible for Medicare. Her mortgage would be paid off, so her debt payments decrease to 0. In addition, household expenses remain the same. Her travel expenses have increased to $10,000. Her total income is $80,000 and total spending is $73,000, resulting in a cash flow of $7,000, which leaves her a cushion should any unexpected expenses arise.

Cash Flow—Age 65

	You	Partner	Combined
Income			
W-2			
Business			
Social Security	30,000		
Rental			
Pension			
Investment	50,000		
Other			
Total Income (I)	80,000		**$ 80,000**
Deductions			
Tax	10,000		
Retirement Contributions	0		
Medical	3,000		
Household	50,000		
Travel	10,000		
Other			
Total Deductions (D)			**$ 73,000**
Debt Payments (P)			**$ 0**
D + P = S			**$ 73,000**
Cash Flow (I − S)		80,000 − 73,000	**$ 7,000**

Now it's time for you to project your future cash flow. Use the information you gathered from your Simplified Cash Flow Analysis and Data Gathering Forms to complete your Proposed Future Cash Flow Analysis Form. At the bottom of the form, subtract your total spending from your total income. The result is your projected cash flow.

Congratulations! You have a completed a Proposed Future Cash Flow Analysis and are on your way to becoming part of the 25 percent of people who complete a financial plan. Please be aware that this is a SIMPLIFIED example that does not account for inflation. If you'd like help in calculating a more exact computation, contact a financial planner or one of our Certified Guides, who are trained in this process.

Proposed Future Cash Flow Analysis Form

	You	*Partner*	*Combined*
Income			
W-2			
Business			
Social Security			
Rental			
Pension			
Investment			
Other			
Total Income (I)			$ _____
Deductions			
Tax			
Retirement Contributions			
Medical			
Household			
Travel			
Other			
Total Deductions (D)			$ _____
Debt Payments (P)			$ _____
D + P = S			$ _____
Cash Flow (I − S)			$ _____

Are there gaps between what you thought you had spent and what you actually spent? Don't be shocked if you spent more than you had thought. Almost everyone underestimates their spending. I did, and I've been doing this professionally for twenty-five years.

Knowing how much you spend enables you to make adjustments to free up additional cash, if necessary. For example, the amount my wife and I spent dining out was much higher than I had thought, so we reduced the number of times we dined out. It was that simple.

In addition, if you discover that your savings from income doesn't equal the amount of money you should have in the bank, based on your income minus your expenses, review your Data

Gathering Form in appendix 2. You can adjust the cash flow—and your expenses—to reflect your actual spending.

Soon, we'll learn how to use your completed Current Cash Flow Analysis to live your ideal life.

But first, let's see how the husband and wife who wanted to sail the Mediterranean for a month made that happen. Before they could determine how to finance the trip, they had to figure out how much the trip would cost—approximately $25,000—and when they wanted to take the trip—in four years.

When looking at their Current Cash Flow Analysis, we determined they didn't have enough money in their budget to fund both the trip and their current retirement plan. They could either save for the trip or delay their retirement for a year. They chose to save for the trip, putting $500 a month into their trip fund over the next four years. Their income didn't change to finance the trip. We simply made adjustments in their budget in order to accommodate it, saving for the trip by reducing their current retirement contributions.

If you really want to do something and you figure out your finances, you can make it happen. You may have to make choices or give something up in order to accomplish what you really want to do, but you can do it. You can live your ideal life and fulfill your purpose. Figuring out your finances is just as important as figuring out your purpose statement. Without this step, you can't make it a reality.

But that's still not enough. You also need to know what's important in your life.

CHAPTER 9

U: Understanding What's Important to Create Your Ideal Life

IF YOU'RE FAMILIAR WITH MCDONALD'S, YOU'RE PROBABLY HEARD OF RAY KROC. ACCORDING TO *TheBalancesMB.com*,[15] Ray described his purpose as inspiring potential, stating, "I like to get people fired up, fill them with zeal for McDonald's, and watch the results in their work." Ray knew what was important to him. Despite great financial success, he worked at McDonald's and lived his ideal life until the day he died.

It all started when Ray was working as a salesman selling milkshake machines to the McDonald's brothers' restaurant in California. The restaurant's success led to Ray's vision, not of hamburgers and French fries, but of a system that consistently delivered the same food and service, whether it was located in Albuquerque or Atlanta. He could see McDonald's potential as a business that

---

15   Don Daszkowski, "Ray Kroc and the McDonald's Phenomenon," The Balances MB, Dotdash Publishing, September 24, 2018, *https://www.thebalancesmb.com/the-ray-kroc-story-mcdonalds-facts-and-history-1350971*.

could deliver results in hundreds of restaurants around the country. So, Ray quit his job as a milkshake machine salesman and joined McDonald's working to bring this vision to fruition. Today, McDonald's has more than 36,000 restaurants in 120 countries.

Ray's original purpose certainly underestimated the potential of McDonald's, but it enabled him to know what he wanted to accomplish. The idea is to picture yourself at your best, fulfilling your life's purpose. There is no risk in exploring new ideas and opportunities that support your purpose, particularly if you're only doing it with a pencil and paper right now.

Allow yourself to envision the life of your dreams. But keep in mind that there is no magic wand to provide immediate access to your ideal future. You will have choices and decisions to make. Remember the Mediterranean sailors? In order to fulfill their purpose of discovery and exploration, and to create their ideal life, they chose to delay their retirement so they could finance the trip.

Knowing what's important in your life is key to creating your ideal life. For Ray Kroc it was getting others excited about McDonald's. For the Mediterranean sailors, it was visiting areas that place happiness above material wealth and considering how to help sustain and protect those areas for future generations.

Ask yourself: What do I want in my ideal future? What's important to me?

Where Are You Coming From?

In thinking about your future, it's important to understand where you're coming from.

The letter "F" in the word "from" stands for family and friends, "R" for recreation, "O" for occupation, and "M" for money. Let's take a closer look at these elements and why they're important to focus on when creating your ideal life.

F = Family and Friends

One key to successfully transitioning to a life of purpose is surrounding yourself with people who care about you, and people you care about. They encourage you to move toward your ideal life, because these relationships matter.

An ongoing adult development study[16] that began in 1938 at Harvard University followed the lives of eight hundred men for over seventy years and continues to follow both the participants who are still alive and their families. The study's researcher, George Vaillant, discovered that "the capacity for warm, empathetic relationships is the strongest predictor of health, wealth, happiness, and satisfaction." And he summed it up by stating, "The only thing that really matters in life are your relationships with other people."

So, ask yourself the following questions:

---

16   Liz Mineo, "Good Genes Are Nice, but Joy Is Better," *Harvard Gazette*, April 11, 2017, *https://news.harvard. edu/gazette/story/2017/04/over-nearly-80-years-harvard-study-has-been-showing-how-to-live-a-healthy-and-happy-life/.*

1. Which relationships are important in your ideal future?

2. Whom do you know, or know of, who could help you achieve your vision?

3. Whom do you currently have a relationship with who could help you?

4. Whom do you currently have a relationship with who can be of help, who has a different set of skills than you, but who shares your beliefs?

Sharing your purpose with others is a critical part of finding people who share your beliefs. That's where you'll find followers, partners, potential coworkers or employees, and friends who will help you bring your purpose to the world.

R = Recreation

Recreation is an important part of your life. It brings you joy, adds fun to your life, and gives you something to look forward to doing with friends and family, or by yourself if that's what you enjoy. In creating your ideal life, it's important to understand which activities you love doing so that you can find ways to continue doing them.

Ask yourself the following questions:

1. What do you currently do for fun?

2. What are your favorite activities, and what do you love about them?

3. Who joins you in your favorite activities?

4. What do you do to stay healthy?

5. When living your ideal life, how many vacations do you plan to take each year, and with whom?

6. Where will you go?

7. What about these places is appealing to you?

8. What do you love about the city or town where you live now?

9. What do you love about your neighborhood and your home?

10. Would you change any or all of those things?

You're probably wondering why the above questions and answers are important. Let's look at Steve Davis,[17] who, along with his wife and two daughters, has a very active lifestyle enjoying

---

17   The name and details of this story have been changed to protect the privacy of the individual involved; however, the story illustrates the point of what happened.

outdoor sports and recreation. At least once a year, sometimes twice, they'll take a big ski trip to Europe or Canada and spend several weeks skiing. They also take a big rafting trip—or some other adventure trip—once or twice a year.

Steve loves reconnecting with his family in beautiful locations, uninterrupted by real life. It's reinvigorating to enjoy the things he loves and to pass on that enthusiasm to his wife and kids.

Although Steve lives in the house he wants to live in and likes his community, he also relishes the ability to travel to places where he can enjoy the sports that he loves.

O = Occupation

Let's look at your occupation now. Understanding which aspects of your work that you enjoy and which you would change will help you move toward living your ideal life. It's also important to recognize what financial constraints tie you to your current work.

Again, ask yourself these questions:

1. What do you love about what you do right now?

1. Does your current work allow you to live your purpose?

2. Does any part of what you do allow you to live your ideal life? For most people, living their ideal life all day every day isn't possible due to financial constraints. But is it possible to transform any part of what you're doing right now into living your ideal life?

Let's see how Phillip Miller made changes to live his ideal life. Phillip and his wife are doctors and partners in a general practitioner medical team. Medical practice in general has become incredibly demanding and time-consuming. He knew in his soul that primary care wasn't working for him, and despite ongoing efforts to make it work, it was like putting "a round peg in a square hole." It was killing him.

When Phillip's wife became sick and was unable to work, it put even more pressure on Phillip. Eventually, he stopped working, taking a year to reevaluate his life and his purpose, figuring out what brought him joy, and determining what talents he had that would enable him to help others.

One day, Phillip woke up with an epiphany, realizing that many dermatology patients were referred out of his community for treatment. He always enjoyed using his medical knowledge and skills in dermatology, so he decided to approach a local medical group and ask if they would be willing to create an avenue for him to practice dermatology. At first, they were hesitant, but they finally agreed.

Now, instead of working approximately eighty hours a week as a general practitioner, Phillip works twenty-eight hours a week as a dermatologist. In the short period of time since he made the change, he has diagnosed fourteen cases of early-stage melanoma, saving fourteen lives. Instead of being drained at work, Phillip enjoys his work more deeply. He's invigorated and energized because his heart and passion are in dermatology.

If your current work won't allow you to live your purpose, if no matter how you look at your job you're just working for the money, or if you're accepting high levels of stress and long hours, you need to consider an alternative. But that's a big step. Instead of quitting your day job, list three to five occupations or businesses that would support your purpose. These should be specific and realistic, enabling you to earn the money it takes to pay the bills. You may need additional education, which you would need to build into your plan, or you may be able to shift into a new position without additional education.

What would it take to shift into each of the three to five ideas you had? For example, remember Ed, the sheriff who found a calling in the religious world that didn't pay nearly as much as his sheriff job. To make the shift and to be able to meet his financial obligations, he took a job providing private security for a family in addition to working as a deacon.

M = Money

When I ask people what their ideal income would be, most state an enormous number. But that's not realistic. Keeping the Millard Fuller story in mind, think about how much money you need to support your ideal life. The easiest way to determine that is to look at your cash flow analysis. For most people, the amount of money you'll need in order to keep your cash flow the same will be higher than your current level of income. For some, it might be lower, like the doctor who changed jobs to work in dermatology and reduced his hours. He made up the difference by drawing income from his savings and investments. Although his working income declined as a result of a smaller paycheck, the job change allowed him to lead a less stressful life and his overall cash flow remained the same.

Referring back to your Current Cash Flow Analysis, make an educated guess about the costs associated with living your ideal life and fulfilling your purpose—retiring, changing jobs, taking vacations, moving, buying a new house, starting a business, etc.—and add or subtract those costs from your current expenses.

Completing the Investment Assets Form will prevent you from making false projections and overestimating your investment income. Complete the form on the next page to bring your savings and investments into the picture.

Be aware that living your ideal life may create an increase or decrease in cash flow. For example, if you decrease your work hours in pursuit of your purpose, it will result in a reduction in income. Or, if pursuing your purpose costs money, you might incur an additional $1,000 a month in expenses. We need to find a way to fill that gap. Your options are to either earn an additional $1,000, reduce expenses by $1,000, or reallocate spending. For example, reduce spending by $200 a month and reduce retirement contributions by $800 a month. If you reduce retirement contributions, however, it may have an impact on when you can retire. These are big decisions, but you have to find the additional $1,000 per month—so you either make more money, spend less, or reallocate. In addition, if you are spending money on items that don't support your purpose, you will need to

Investment Assets Form

Identify all the resources you have to fund your goals. Reasonable estimates are fine.

You

Investment Type	Current Value, $	Annual Additions, $ or %
Retirement Plans (e.g., 401(k), 403b)		
Employer Match		
Traditional IRA		
Roth IRA		
529 Savings Plan		
Annuities		
HSA		
Taxable/Brokerage		
Cash Value Life Insurance		
Real Estate		
Other		

Partner

Investment Type	Current Value, $	Annual Additions, $ or %
Retirement Plans (e.g., 401(k), 403b)		
Employer Match		
Traditional IRA		
Roth IRA		
529 Savings Plan		
Annuities		
HSA		
Taxable/Brokerage		
Cash Value Life Insurance		
Real Estate		
Other		

figure out how to increase income or decrease those expenses. And, if there's anything you should be spending money on that you're not, you will need to figure out how to budget for those expenses.

For most people, some type of financial investment will be necessary to finance their ideal life. And that means investing with confidence.

CHAPTER 10

I: Invest with Confidence to Achieve Your Ideal Life

I FIRST MET CHRIS SKYLAR,[18] THE NEPHEW OF A FAMILY FRIEND, WHILE HE WAS STILL IN HIGH SCHOOL. Like most teenage boys, he enjoyed school sports, girls, and cars. But his real passion was music.

Chris played guitar in the high school jazz band and also formed a band with a few friends. He always wanted to be a professional musician, but he concluded that was something he couldn't pursue, although he still continued to dream about it. Immediately after graduating high school, he went to work for the sheriff's department.

On his days off, Chris continued to play music with his band. As time passed and the group grew older, the band dissolved—and so did Chris's dream of being a professional musician. At the same time, his interest in police work began to wane.

Chris took a job at a local concrete business, and his good nature and work ethic earned him a following at work. Within a few years he was managing the plant. When the plant owner moved to another location, leaving some equipment behind, Chris worked with the landowner, retained the location, and went into business for himself using the existing buildings and equipment.

Because of the relationships Chris had built, his business was successful. After a few years, his former employer closed up his shop, and all his business moved to Chris's business.

---

18   The name and details of this story have been changed to protect the privacy of the individual involved; however, the story illustrates the point of what happened.

Over these next several years, Chris and I worked together to improve his business and personal cash flow, and to create an ideal life experience. Although he originally didn't know what that would look like, Chris began to figure out that it was something in music. It took him approximately a year to lay the foundation for what the future looked like for him, which included getting the money in place in order to make a move.

As profits grew and cash flow increased, Chris invested and built a substantial net worth. The value of his business increased as well. In his mid-forties, Chris sold the business, invested an additional $3 million into his investment plan, and enrolled in college and obtained a degree in music.

Chris now works with high school bands and writes music for school bands. His writing has become popular across the country, and he enjoys royalties that continue in perpetuity and enhance his cash flow. Chris has acquired True Wealth and lives his ideal life.

Now remember, the goal of True Wealth is to create enough resources to pursue your purpose without running out of money. Like Chris, you'll need to increase cash flow and invest for your ideal future.

Since money and investing can be a big stress point for many people, this chapter is dedicated to investing with confidence.

How I Use My Motifs, Values, and Themes to Live My Ideal Life

Remember that list of motifs you discovered after telling your stories to your helper in chapter 4? Let's bring those back into focus, along with the values you've identified, and use them to create the beliefs and investing philosophy that will enable you to pursue your ideal life.

For me, the values that fit are authenticity, dependability, responsibility, gratitude, optimism, learning, wisdom, perseverance, potential, peacefulness, exploration, discovery, improvement, and results-oriented. From those I came up with four important motifs. The first was wisdom, which for me means to see other perspectives and to use insight to guide others. The second was gratitude. The third was results-oriented. And the fourth was optimism, and by optimism, I mean to believe in a better future.

My motifs led to creating the core beliefs and philosophy that went into my business. For example, results-orientated has led me to spend twenty-five years finding investments that provided results for my clients in terms of rising income and rising values. Optimism and the belief that the world will progress over time, that it will become a better and more productive place, and that humans will solve big problems with innovation (eliminating the need for fossil fuels or curing the flu, for example) is a real driver in my ability to invest with confidence for the past twenty-five years, and my company's getting better results than the vast majority of the population.

My motifs have enabled me to create an investment philosophy, which has led to me to live my ideal life by helping others find their purpose and unlock their potential.

Let's take a look at how these core beliefs tie into investing.

Investing Core Beliefs

At my company, we have three core beliefs. The first is that the world will progress over time and become better and more productive. If you look at Gross Domestic Product (GDP), which measures all economic activity and is the sum of market values or prices of all finished goods and services during a period of time, the current annual American GDP is six times what it was in 1930. Do people work six times harder? Are they six times smarter? No, they're just more efficient and able to produce more. Human innovation—electricity, motorized transportation, and computer technology, for example—impacted productivity.

The historical growth rate of the U.S. economy is approximately 2 percent per year. Because the population grows at about .8 percent a year, this results in a per capita GDP growth of 1.2 percent (2 percent economic growth rate minus .8 percent population growth). If you compound that annual growth for the next generation, it results in a gain of 34.4 percent or a $19,000 gain in income per person, and $76,000 gain in income for a family of four. A typical middle-class family today enjoys a better standard of living (transportation, medical services, entertainment, and communication, etc.) than Henry Ford did in the 1930s.

My company's second core belief is having an optimistic view of the future and extraordinary faith in human potential. It's the only realistic choice. Human potential and ingenuity—semiconductors, penicillin, optical lenses, and the printing press, to name a few—have solved problems and changed the course of history. In the future, driverless flying cars, space colonies, autonomous robots, and the elimination of the need for fossil fuels will create additional changes.

Our third core belief is that we can individually create the future of our choosing by embracing human progress and innovation rather than fearing it. This allows us to far exceed typical investor results.

Avoiding Investing Mistakes

Nobody's perfect, but investors, as a group, tend to make the same mistakes over and over. Let's look at some of the common mistakes that hurt your ability to achieve an acceptable return on your investments.

1. Attempting to time the market. Most investors fail to achieve anything close to the performance of the market. Data analysis firm DALBAR's studies show that the average investor's returns have been close to 50 percent of the return of the unmanaged S&P 500 index. Over the trailing thirty-year period, the average stock mutual fund investor earned 60 percent less than the index. Investor temperament is to blame, and the belief that they can consistently guess the direction of the market. The problem is that they often guess wrong.

2. Short-term focus makes you your own worst enemy. The common mistake is to buy hot recent market performers and then move on to the next top performer when the first lags.

3. Moving to cash when you fear a market decline. According to legendary money manager Peter Lynch[19] (he managed the Fidelity Magellan fund from 1977 to 1990 and averaged a 29.2 percent average annual return), "Far more money has been lost by investors preparing for corrections, or trying to anticipate corrections, than has been lost in the corrections themselves."

4. Investing in the "next big thing" such as the cure for cancer or the common cold. Attempting to "get in on the ground floor" has created many more strikeouts than grand slams.

5. Never starting, or quitting, investing because you believe it doesn't work. If you quit investing, your cash flow will be completely derived from your current working income. At some point if you plan to quit working, there's nothing there to fill in that gap. This will limit your ability to live your ideal life, because you'll be focused on creating enough income to cover your expenses.

Rules for Successful Investing

If you want to achieve your ideal life, you need to generate as much investment income as possible so that you won't have to work so hard to pay the bills and can focus on fulfilling your purpose. In order to do that you must:

1. Have an investing plan.

2. Invest with confidence by buying quality investments and holding them for a long period of time.

3. Don't put time and energy into guessing the direction of the next 15 percent move in the market when we absolutely know that the next 100 percent move is up. Don't let the news of the day drive your investment decisions.

4. Focus on cash flow and work to optimize it.

5. Keep enough cash on hand to cover current spending needs so that you won't need to sell investments when, and not if, they go down.

6. Never be all in or all out. There is no surer way to fail in investing than trying to time the market. It's no wonder that investor's try—the "experts" in the financial media would have you believe that the only way to make money is by correctly guessing the next 15 percent move in the market. Successful investing does not require clairvoyance.

7. Diversify between asset classes (cash, bonds, or stocks). It's the best protection from overconfidence or fear.

---

19   Ben Carlson, "Peter Lynch on Stock Market Losses," *A Wealth of Common Sense*, August 2, 2014, *awealthofcommonsense.com*.

8. Instead of speculating on the next big thing, buy proven industry leaders when they regularly go on sale. For example, during market declines in 2015, shares of Microsoft fell below $40 per share. Today, they trade at $190 per share—that's a 250 percent increase. During that same period, Amazon shares were available for under $400, and today they trade at $2180 per share—that's a 445 percent increase. Proven, established market leaders, purchased at a reduced price, produce strong portfolio returns.

9. Invest in companies that provide a rising income from dividends. You'll be less sensitive to market declines when the investments you own continue to provide additional income every year and improve your cash flow. For example, in 2002, I purchased 1,000 shares of Corning each for several of my clients for a little over $1,500. Corning is the same company that made your grandma's dishes, but they also make fiberglass, fiber optic cable, and all things glass. As of July 2019, those shares are worth $40,144.11. The company now pays a 2.4 percent dividend, and the yield on the original investment is 61.7 percent, meaning my clients get 61.7 percent of their original investment back every year. That's the power of rising dividends. That's the power of buying a quality company and continuing to own it when the media experts told you to sell.

Perhaps the facts above fail to persuade you. You may feel like my friend, successful small businessman Collin Stewart. He's concerned that the next economic downturn or total financial collapse is right around the corner. Facts alone do not overcome fear, only trust does. To Collin, and all of you who don't share my optimism, I offer the following guidance, again from the legendary Peter Lynch:

If you had invested $1,000 on the lowest day in the market each and every year for the 30-year period from 1965 to 1995, "you would have earned an average annual return of 11.7 percent. On the flip side, if you had invested at the market high of each year, your return would have been 10.6 percent. Finally, if you had simply invested $1000 at the beginning of every year, you would have earned 11.0 percent per year." To recap: Perfect market timing produced 11.7 percent, horrible timing returns were 10.6 percent, and no market timing resulted in 11.0 percent. Either way, that's better than you would have done by not investing! When you invest you do need to be prepared for times of volatility. There have always been and will always be reasons to be concerned.[20]

If you don't know how to invest on your own, enlist the help of your financial advisor, or go to our website (*truewealthguide.net*) and let one of our financial guides help you.

Investing with confidence helps you achieve your ideal life by providing you with a rising income that you can't outlive. When you stop working and the paychecks no longer come in, there will be a gap between how much you spend and how much income you receive from Social Security and/or your pension. Investments are there to fill that gap and provide the income that allows you to pursue your purpose and live your life without having to work.

---

20 Peter Lazaroff, "Time Beats Timing," Bright Plan, August 15, 2019, *https://www.brightplan.com/blog/time-beats-timing*.

But if you're like most people, you don't have a financial plan in place. In the next chapter, I'll show you how to figure out the finances.

CHAPTER 11

D: Developing the Financial Plan to Live the Life of Your Choice

ROBBIE BURNS KNEW HIS PURPOSE LONG BEFORE WE STARTED WORKING ON HIS PLAN. WHEN HE WAS eleven years old, as he watched ski and snowboard racers, he knew he wanted to go fast. Like most eleven-year-olds, he had big dreams.

Robbie wanted to compete in the Olympics as a snowboarder. He wanted to be the best in the world and to stand on the podium and receive a medal. Robbie told his family about his goals and worked toward his dream. He continued to improve his skills and began to win more and more races.

After a big win in Colorado, a reporter asked Robbie about his plans. That was the first time Robbie let the world know that he was headed to the Olympics. But Robbie's purpose is bigger than going to the Olympics. Robbie's purpose is to live a life that inspires people to take bold steps on their path with kindness, courage, and compassion in the hope that we will all share the love and interconnectedness that has always been present but not always expressed.

Robbie's purpose has given him the power to push through difficulties and obstacles. When he missed the Seoul, South Korea, Olympics—the United States took two snowboarders and Robbie was the third best—he kept training during the day while working nights as a security guard five days a week, leaving only a few hours a day for sleep. Robbie's schedule was not ideal for anyone, particularly not for an athlete in training. But Robbie had to work; U.S. Olympic athletes are not supported by the government, unlike athletes in some other countries.

Knowing it can easily cost $50,000 to $90,000 a year to train as a world-class snowboarder, we began to put together a financial plan, focusing on Robbie's goal of snowboarding at the 2022 Beijing Olympics and of inspiring others.

Now, instead of working nights as a security guard during the winter while he's snowboarding, Robbie works as a hotshot firefighter in the summers, making between $9,000 and $25,000. The remainder of the income he needs to train is obtained from fundraisers and corporate sponsorships.

Robbie states that having a financial plan in place and not having to work forty hours a week while training six hours a day makes it easier to focus on his training and his goals. He now has time to speak to children and adults about his purpose and about snowboarding. In addition, he's moved from ranking 300th in the world to 15th.

I can see the determination in Robbie's eyes. Look for him on the podium in 2022; he's going to be there.

Ideal Life Financial Plan

Lack of money has derailed a lot of dreams. You must begin with the end in mind, which is creating enough income to fulfill your purpose and live your ideal life.

Here is a useful device to estimate investment income: $1.6 million at a 6 percent return will provide $100,000 a year in income and allow a 2.5 percent per year cost of living increase. So, if you need to make $50,000 per year in income from investments, you need half of $1.6 million or $800,000 in savings.

Let's bring back our fifty-five-year-old planner from chapter 8. Let's give her a name and a purpose. Amy has successfully reentered the workforce after raising her children, working as a staff attorney for a benefits and human resources company. Her purpose is to equip women with the essential tools needed to reenter the workforce in order to help women worldwide realize their value.

She plans to create a digital training and employment company within five years. After sharing her purpose with friends, coworkers, and associates at other firms whom she has relationships with through her current job, she's found the support and financing needed to make it happen.

She currently earns $100,000 per year, has $300,000 in her 401(k), and plans to make the transition to her business at age sixty. Her sample ideal life cash flow below details her current income and expenses as well as her projection at age sixty.

In the five years from age fifty-five to age sixty, her retirement assets from investing grew to $500,000. Using our $1.6 million formula from earlier, Amy's $500,000 would safely provide up to $32,000 of income. Her plan is to supplement her $76,000 salary from her business with $24,000 from her retirement savings. Since her income and expenses remain the same, Amy proceeds with confidence.

	Age 55	Age 60
Income		
W-2	100,000	76,000*
Business		
Social Security		
Rental		
Pension		
Investment		24,000
Other		
Total Income (I)	**100,000**	**100,000**
Deductions		
Tax	20,000	20,000
Retirement Contributions	15,000	15,000
Medical	3,000	3,000
Household	50,000	50,000
Travel	2,000	2,000
Other		
Total Deductions (D)	**90,000**	**90,000**
Debt Payments (P)	**10,000**	**10,000**
D + P	**100,000**	**100,000**
Total Investment Value*	**300,000**	**500,000**

Plus the potential of profits

If you want to live your ideal life, you now need to figure out how much money you'll need by completing the Ideal Life Plan Form. Remember to start with your end goal in mind, your ideal life, by describing it in the space provided. Determine when you want to retire and how your expenses will likely change as they did for Amy. Maybe you want to buy a second house in a warmer climate, travel more, or open a dance studio. If your plan is to work part-time, add the additional income into your plan.

	You	Partner	Combined
Income			
W-2			
Business			
Social Security			
Rental			
Pension			
Investment			
Other			
Total Income (I)			$ _____
Deductions			
Tax			
Retirement Contributions			
Medical			
Household			
Travel			
Other			
Total Deductions (D)			$ _____
Debt Payments (P)			$ _____
D + P = S			$ _____
Cash Flow (I − S)			$ _____

If, after completing the form, you determine you won't have enough income to finance your ideal life, think about how you can make changes—it's important to make sure you get to eat lunch today and when you're ninety. For example, if you want to buy a second house in a warmer climate, you can consider renting a house for a few months instead of buying, which will save you money. Or if you want to retire sooner rather than later, maybe you decide to own one home instead of two. You may go through ten scenarios before you select the one that's best for you, but keep your options open and think outside the box.

Investment Assets Form

Identify all the resources you have to fund your goals. Reasonable estimates are fine.

You

Investment Type	Current Value, $	Annual Additions, $ or %
Retirement Plans (e.g., 401(k), 403b)		
Employer Match		
Traditional IRA		
Roth IRA		
529 Savings Plan		
Annuities		
HSA		
Taxable/Brokerage		
Cash Value Life Insurance		
Real Estate		
Other		

Partner

Investment Type	Current Value, $	Annual Additions, $ or %
Retirement Plans (e.g., 401(k), 403b)		
Employer Match		
Traditional IRA		
Roth IRA		
529 Savings Plan		
Annuities		
HSA		
Taxable/Brokerage		
Cash Value Life Insurance		
Real Estate		
Other		

Robbie the snowboarder, who had a really compelling purpose, sacrificed in order to keep his purpose alive. Putting a financial plan together and executing it took so much pressure off him that his snowboarding performance improved and continues to improve.

Like Robbie, the financial plans you draw up are going to require some choices in order to make them work. For most people, the available cash flow doesn't work with their plan, particularly if they'd like to retire tomorrow.

Questions to Ask Yourself as You Build Your Ideal Life

1. Do you live where you want to live?

2. Are you living your purpose?

3. If you are not living your purpose, are you getting closer to it?

4. If your income won't be enough to allow you to live your ideal life, how can you resolve it? Brainstorm five to ten ways to reduce your expenses or increase your income, then determine which are your best options, which are tolerable, which aren't, and which are closest to living your ideal life.

5. Will you have enough financial flexibility to cover unforeseen expenses, such as needing a new vehicle, having a health problem, needing a new roof, or lending your kids money? Make sure you have a cushion for these expenses, roughly 10 percent of income not spent.

Implementing Your Plan

Now that you've completed your Ideal Life Financial Plan Form and asked yourself some tough questions, it's time to put your plan to work and put your energy toward living your purpose.

What changes need to be made in order to execute your plan and move toward living your ideal life? What's the first step you need to take? List it here.

_____

List the rest of the steps you need to take in order to achieve your plan, financial and purpose-driven. For example, if you're Robbie and you want to go to the Beijing Olympics in 2022, you need to figure out how to increase corporate sponsorships. Don't forget to build any additional expenses into your plan. If you need more space, use a separate piece of paper, but only list the things you think are important to address at this time.

1. _____

2. _____

3. _____

4. _____

Now put those steps into action.

As you can see, financial planning is a key aspect of living your ideal life, and it's not as difficult as you thought.

Knowing how to achieve True Wealth is just a chapter away.

CHAPTER 12

E: Evaluating and Evolving

THINGS WILL CHANGE, IN THE WORLD IN GENERAL AND IN YOUR LIFE SPECIFICALLY—AND YOU NEED TO be willing to change too.

It's important to evaluate your financial situation and make adjustments as needed.

When creating your ideal life plan, you will make some assumptions that you don't know the specific answers to, such as the rate of return on investments, the inflation rate, or if a curve ball will come into your life and change your situation. For example, you or a family member could become sick, or the pursuit of your purpose could create a significant increase in cash flow. Each factor can change your outcome. If the factors are negative, such as a health problem or a poor rate of return on investments, you won't achieve your ideal life and acquire True Wealth. In order to stay on track, you must make adjustments as life changes.

Let's look at how to do that.

How to Evaluate and Evolve Your Finances

I reevaluate my clients' plans (and my own) at least annually, unless significant changes occur sooner than a year. You should do the same.

Look at your Ideal Life Financial Plan Form and determine if income, expenses, or investment results could alter the outcome. For example, at thirty-seven years old, Barry decided he wanted to be a motivational speaker for students. The income he earned from speaking events provided him with an additional $50,000 a year beyond the salary he made working as an NFL referee. Travel expenses to the speaking engagements equaled $10,000, resulting in an overall cash flow increase of $40,000 a year. This increase in cash flow gave Barry the option to reduce the hours he worked as an NFL referee and to put more energy—and perhaps even all of his energy—toward his new purpose-driven life.

In making his decision, Barry asked himself the following questions:

1. Would it be feasible to completely shift my work to make motivational speaking my primary source of income? If so, when can I do it?

2. Does giving speeches make me feel like I'm living the ideal life I had envisioned? (If Barry's answer is no, he needs to reevaluate his purpose by asking what's different than he thought it would be, and why. He also needs to decide if he's getting something positive from giving speeches that he hadn't expected.)

3. Am I financially prepared to make motivational speaking my vocation and my purpose?

4. What does motivational speaking mean to me in terms of who I am and how I want my life to be?

If Barry quit his job and earned $40,000 a year after expenses as a motivational speaker, his finances would be tight. He decides to cut back his hours and work fewer games in order to earn the additional income he needs to live comfortably.

Now, what if Barry's mom has a medical problem and he contributes financially to help her? This isn't an expense he had anticipated.

In this scenario, Barry asks himself the following questions to determine how he can continue to fulfill his purpose and live his ideal life:

1. How can I reevaluate my ideal life under this new set of circumstances to make it fit my changed financial situation?

2. What does my ideal life plan look like in this new situation?

3. What changes do I need to make in terms of what I do every day in order to finance my ideal life? Can I reduce spending on entertainment, get a better-paying job, not eat out as much?

Because Barry is unable to save as much money as he had thought, he decides to work full-time for two additional years while saving the funds he needs to enable him to work solely as a motivational speaker.

Let's look at another example of how to evaluate and evolve.

Geri wants to set up an orphanage in Guatemala that will require her to be away from her job for an extended period of time. In addition to obtaining funding for the orphanage, Geri has to find a way to replace her income, so she organizes fundraisers. Because the fundraisers are successful, the orphanage becomes a reality. However, Geri needs an ongoing influx of money to continue to fund the orphanage, so she returns annually to the United States to organize fundraisers in her hometown. Soon, Guatemala recognizes the orphanage's importance and starts to contribute financially.

Geri asks herself the following questions to determine how she can continue to fulfill her purpose and live her ideal life:

1. Can I rely on the Guatemalan government to continue to support the orphanage, enabling me to quit fundraising and focus full-time on the orphanage?

2. What aspects of what I'm doing would I change, if any?

3. Is running an orphanage as fulfilling as I had hoped?

4. If I cut back or stop my fundraising efforts, what happens if the Guatemalan government cuts its funding to the orphanage?

5. If I cease my fundraising efforts and need to start fundraising again, will I be able to get back in the game and raise money?

6. If the orphanage were to lose its funding, what other resources exist, and how could I build the relationships to acquire those funds?

Geri decides it's best to focus on the now, knowing she has the necessary skills and contacts she needs should it be necessary to raise funds for the orphanage in the future. The funding that the orphanage receives from the government enables Geri to reduce her fundraising efforts in the United States, makes the orphanage less reliant on the kindness of Geri's community, and allows Geri to focus her efforts on running the orphanage rather than on fundraising.

But what if Geri arrives in Guatemala to set up the orphanage and discovers she isn't getting the support she needs from the local government? In fact, they're making it difficult and charging her fees that she hadn't expected.

Questions Geri asks herself, intent on fulfilling her purpose by creating a successful orphanage, are:

1. Am I willing to spend time fundraising in United States?

2. What resources do I have to pursue?

3. Can I cut back on expenses at the orphanage?

4. Can I build a smaller orphanage than I envisioned?

Because Geri feels she is the best person to oversee setting up the orphanage and because she doesn't want to spend time away from it, she decides to build a smaller orphanage than she had intended with the hopes of expanding it in the future. She will evaluate her finances on an annual basis to see if she's on track to meet her goal, determining what adjustments need to be made to stay on track or to accelerate it.

Now it's time for you to ask:

1. If I need additional income, are there alternative sources I haven't tapped? If so, how can I tap them?

2. Whom do I know or know of who could be helpful in creating another avenue of revenue?

3. How can I reduce spending?

4. Is it time to move toward full pursuit of my purpose rather than keeping my day job and pursuing my purpose part-time?

5. If I quit my day job, will I have enough money to pay my bills?

6. If I'm already pursuing my purpose, is it financially sustainable? If not, what changes do I need to make?

How you evaluate and evolve will be dependent upon your personal situation. What's important is to remember to evaluate your financial plan, either annually or more often, and make adjustments when necessary.

Now that you know how to evaluate and evolve your finances and why it's so important to reevaluate your ideal life financial plan and make adjustments when necessary, you should be actively pursuing your purpose and ideal life. It's not easy, but it's achievable.

CONCLUSION
Living the Plan

THE ROUTE FROM YOUR PRESENT (CURRENT LIFE) TO YOUR FUTURE (IDEAL LIFE) WILL INVOLVE CHANGE. Change can be hard, but science can help. There are three principles that drive change.

1. Social Incentives—Those who surround you with a community of support will help you overcome obstacles and challenges. Robbie, the snowboarder who narrowly missed in his first shot at the Olympics, had incredible support from family, friends, coaches, and therapists who encouraged him to keep pursuing his dream. Because of that support (and Robbie's drive to succeed), his purpose is still alive.

2. Progress Monitoring—What gets measured gets done where progress is highlighted. Creating a scoreboard that measures actions and highlights your progress, rather than one that measures inaction and highlights your regressions, will produce positive future results. As an example, San Francisco gym owner Mystie Hansen has created a scoring system for her group of exercise enthusiasts. They receive one point for every eight hours of sleep, one point for each sixteen ounces of water consumed, and one point for every ten minutes of exercise. They deduct one point for each alcoholic or sugary beverage, and deduct again for dessert. The point is to create a baseline and improve on it. They report scores weekly. That keeps them focused on their health and fitness.

3. Immediate Rewards—Studies show that people will choose something they want or need now over something that might happen in the future.

Weight Watchers is a great example that uses all three principles to drive change and create success. Created more than fifty years ago, Weight Watchers has outlasted many fad diets because the participants create a community of support; they are in it together and encourage each other to stick with their diet plans (Principle Number One—Social Incentives). Each participant monitors his or her progress and is given points for making healthy choices and for using portion control (Principle Number Two—Progress Monitoring). And the Weight Watchers program rewards participants immediately with extra points when they meet their goals, points they can use all at once or over time (Principle Number Three—Immediate Rewards).

As you work to put your purpose into action, build a support community—family, friends, and others who believe in what you want to achieve. Monitor your progress and focus on what matters by creating a point system related to your purpose. For example, give yourself one point for each time you communicate your purpose to somebody new, one point for every ten minutes you rework your purpose, two points for each person you add to your community of support, and one point for every fifteen minutes you work on your purpose and put it into action. Create an immediate reward for achieving your goals, something simple like a coffee, a hike, or a shopping spree, as long as it doesn't interfere with the financial part of fulfilling your purpose.

If you understand your purpose, your potential, and your ideal life, and you implement a strategic financial plan, you can achieve True Wealth.

In closing, let's look at how John O'Leary achieved True Wealth.

In January 1987, nine-year-old John O'Leary learned the hard way why you shouldn't play with matches. As he'd watched some older boys light fires the day before, John lit a small fire on a piece of cardboard and poured gas on it. But the can was too heavy for him to handle. It ignited and exploded, saturating John's clothes with gas and throwing him against the wall—John was on fire.

John ran into the house screaming. His older brother Jim tackled him, wrapped him in a rug, and put out the fire. But the damage had already been done; John had burns on 100 percent of his body, 87 percent of them third degree. As the ambulance drove John away, he could see his brothers and sisters standing on the lawn, and the smoke from the fire pouring out of the garage.

At the hospital, doctors told John's parents that he wouldn't make it. Unaware of that conversation, John, aching with pain and feeling scared, looked at his mom and, in a trembling voice, asked, "Mommy, am I going to die?" He was hoping she would tell him everything would be okay.

John's mom took his hand, reflected for a moment, then said, "John, do you want to die? It's your choice not mine."

John made the choice to live. His mom said, "Take the hand of God. Fight like you've never fought before."

John spent five months in the hospital healing from his burns and the loss of all of his fingers, which had to be amputated. Finally, he returned home and continued to heal, emotionally and physically, wondering if he'd ever have a girlfriend, get married, or be able to work at a job.

After years of rehabilitation, and with the support of his family and his community, John regained control of his body and was able to walk again. He lived his life as normal as possible, which benefited his healing—but it also led him to hide his scars. He covered them physically with clothing and emotionally with humor—and as he grew older, with alcohol.

The fire, the scars, the amputations, and the pain provided a perfect alibi for accepting roadblocks and challenges and kept John from fulfilling his purpose.

Then a woman who led a third-grade Girl Scout troop heard about John's story and was deeply moved. She asked John if he would talk about his life to the girls. That became his first speech. Later that year, John spoke to fourth graders at a local school and then to a local Rotary Club. The next year, he spoke thirteen times, and each time his speech got better, and he became more confident. The more John spoke, the more he felt that was what he was supposed to do.

Once John started sharing his story, he built a remarkable community of supporters who helped him persevere. He also began to see the impact he could have on others' lives. Speaking to others about his story was about the contribution he could make to others, rather than about himself.

"Looking back," John says, "The choices we made would lead either to a life of hope and possibility or to a life of fear and regret. We all make these choices throughout our lives. I hope to open your eyes to help you truly see which path you were choosing to go down. The first choice you must make to ignite a radically inspired life is to own your life. It's to leave entitlement behind and realize that it's up to you to make the changes in your life. You have the responsibility for what happens next in your life. You must go all in each day with a purpose greater than yourself."[21]

John's purpose is to radically inspire lives, to transform lives from ordinary to extraordinary regardless of their circumstances. Now in his forties, John is married to the girl of his dreams, they have four children, and he owns and runs a business, speaking to over 50,000 people per year. The book you are reading now is a practical guide to finding your purpose, while John's book *On Fire* is an inspirational message of hope, resilience, and possibility. John is fulfilling his purpose.

So am I. My purpose is to help my clients live their ideal life and achieve True Wealth. In addition to writing this book, I've created the Financial Guide Service. If you need financial guidance to put your Ideal Life Plan into action, contact your advisor or contact me at *www.truewealthguide.net*. Together, we can create a financial plan that enables you to live your life's purpose and makes the financing work.

What are you waiting for? It's time to fulfill your purpose, live your ideal life, and achieve True Wealth.

---

21 John O'Leary, *On Fire* (New York: Gallery Books, 2016).

APPENDIX 1

Helper Instructions

Thank you for participating in The GUIDE Process; it's critical for your partner. In case he (or she) hasn't filled you in, the word "GUIDE" in The GUIDE Process is an acronym in which the "G" means to gather information, "U" to unlock potential, "I" to identify motifs, "D" to develop your purpose statement, and "E" to evaluate and evolve. Your partner is using The GUIDE Process to find and finance his ideal life and acquire True Wealth. Your role is to help him do that, but before you get started please read the rest of the appendix, so you know how to help.

Your partner will gather stories from his life and share them with you. As you listen, your job will be to ask clarifying questions about how each story contributes to your partner's life, become aware of patterns in the stories, and help identify themes and motifs that will assist your partner in identifying his purpose. You may discover context that they had not identified. It's important to ask open-ended questions rather than those that can be answered with a "yes" or "no." You also should ask questions that focus on your partner's feelings in each story.

Sample questions to ask are:

1. Specifically, what did/didn't you like about what happened?

2. How does that fit into your "big picture?"

3. I heard you say_____. What may I have misunderstood about that story?

4. What made you feel good/bad about that?

5. When that happened, how did it make you feel?

6. What makes this particular story special?

7. How did that experience impact who you have become?

8. What lessons did you learn from that situation that you still carry with you today?

9. What about that situation do you want to carry into your future?

Tips to Make Your Job More Effective

1. It's hard to keep up when people are telling you their stories. They often talk fast and it's easy to forget something. Take shorthand notes about what you're hearing and why it's important. The easiest way to do that is to create five columns on a piece of paper, but feel free to use whatever method works for you.

a. Label the first column "Story," and write a short description that will identify the story and trigger your memory of what that story is about. For example, Olympic tryouts or leaving grandma and grandpa behind.

b. Label the second column "Details," and write an abbreviated version of what happened in the story.

c. Label the third column "Feelings," and identify how your partner felt during the events of the story.

d. Label the fourth column "Action or Value," and note what action your partner took in the story. For example, if the story is about teaching kids how to play soccer, the action is teaching. Or if the story is about giving a speech about overcoming adversity, the action is inspiring or motivating. If an active action does not exist, like being forced to move away from your best friend when you were young, write down what your partner values in the story.

e. Label the fifth column "Impact on Others," and note how the events of the story impacted your partner and others.

6. Be present. Focus on what your partner is saying. Although you'll be hearing about his past, your job is to actively listen to what he's telling you right now.

7. Make good eye contact and show both verbal and nonverbal engagement.

8. Don't interject your views or your perspective of the story. It is not a time to offer solutions.

9. Use your instincts as to when to probe for more details.

10. Be curious and help your partner dig deeper into each story.

11. Summarize each life stage section and try to draw out the most important feelings.

12. Pay attention to your partner's body language and demeanor.

13. If your partner thinks of a new story when telling you another, let him tell the new story too.

14. As the stories flow, you'll start to see repeated words and themes or motifs. Highlight the words that appear more than once.

Once your partner has shared his stories, he will instruct you to move to another room to analyze the stories and identify motifs. You will then rejoin your partner, and he will instruct you further.

APPENDIX 2

Data Gathering Form

Below is the Data Gathering Form, which will provide an approximation of where your expenses and income stand right now. In completing the form, take your time and be as accurate as possible. If you have some or all of the information on a spreadsheet somewhere, transfer it to the form. If you don't know any information, do your best to figure it out. For example, Social Security benefits can be found online at *SSA.gov*. Pension income can be obtained from your employer. Investment values and bank account balances are listed on mailed statements or online accounts.

There are two columns on the form: Current Monthly Budget Amount and Ideal Life/True Wealth Monthly Budget Amount.

Steps for Completing the Form are:

1. Look at each item in the Personal and Family Expenses Category and, if you have an expense associated with that item, list the expense in the current column.

2. List the anticipated expenses for your Ideal Life/True Wealth in the next column. Alimony, if you have it now, is going to cease, for example. Business expenses fall off. Vacation and travel expenses increase.

3. Follow the same process for the Income Category. Be sure to include all your family income, including investment income.

4. If you have disability insurance, life insurance, long-term care insurance, medical insurance, umbrella liability insurance, or any other type of insurance, list those expenses in the Personal Insurance Expenses Category. Don't forget to complete the True Wealth estimations as well.

5. Taxes, those dreaded taxes. Yep, list those too.

6. On the next page are Home Expenses and Vehicle Expenses. There is space for two cars under vehicle expenses. If you have more than two cars, list their expenses too.

Data Gathering Form

	You, *age* ___	**Partner,** *age* ___
Name		
Employment Status	□ Employed □ Retired □ Business Owner □ Homemaker	□ Employed □ Retired □ Business Owner □ Homemaker
Employment Income	$ _____	$ _____
Other Income (non-investment only)	$ _____	$ _____

Retirement Age		
At what age would you like to retire?	You *(e.g., age 65)* _____	Partner *(e.g., age 65, together)* _____

Social Security Benefits – if available, provide your Social Security estimate from ssa.gov		
Are you eligible?	□ Yes □ No □ Receiving Now	□ Yes □ No □ Receiving Now
Benefit Amount	Primary Insurance Amount (PIA) $ _____	Primary Insurance Amount (PIA) $ _____
When to Start	□ at full retirement age (SocSec) □ at age____ □ at retirement	□ at full retirement age (SocSec) □ at age____ □ at retirement

Retirement Income (pension, part-time work, rental property, annuities, royalties, alimony)

Description	Owner Y	Owner P	Monthly Income	Start Year	Year It Ends/ # of Years	% Survivor Benefit	Check If Amount Inflates	Gov't Pension Offset
	□	□	$ _____				□	□
	□	□	$ _____				□	□
	□	□	$ _____				□	□
	□	□	$ _____				□	□
	□	□	$ _____				□	□

Personal and Family Expenses

Category	Monthly Budget	
	Current	**Alternative/Retirement**
Alimony		
Bank Charges		
Books/Magazines		
Business Expense		
Care of Parent/Other		
Cash — Miscellaneous		
Cell Phone		
Charitable Donations		
Child Activities		
Child Allowance/Expense		
Child Care		
Child Support		
Child Tutor		
Clothing — Client		
Clothing — Co-Client		
Clothing — Children		
Club Dues		
Credit Card Debt		
Dining		
Entertainment		
Gifts		
Groceries		
Healthcare—Dental		
Healthcare—Medical		
Household Items		
Laundry/Dry Cleaning		
Personal Care		
Personal Loan Payment		
Pet Care		
Public Transportation		
Recreation		
Self Improvement		
Student Loan		
Vacation/Travel		
Other:		

Home Expenses

Category	Monthly Budget	
	Current	Alternative/Retirement
First Mortgage		
Second Mortgage		
Equity Line		
Real Estate Tax		
Rent		
Homeowners Insurance		
Association Fees		
Electricity		
Gas/Oil		
Trash Pickup		
Water/Sewer		
Cable/HD TV Internet		
Telephone (landline)		
Lawn Care		
Maintenance—Major Repair		
Maintenance—Regular		
Furniture		
Household Help		
Other		

You've completed your Data Gathering Form. Now use it to complete your Current Cash Flow Analysis Form in chapter 8.

ACKNOWLEDGMENTS

Writing a book is something I've wanted to do for decades. It would not have happened without...

My fantastic wife, Robin, who lets me do what I want to do, even coming home to tell her I had bought an airplane! Thanks for the editorial help and for allowing me the time to write.

My daughter, Carey, who unlocked an important part of the puzzle of my purpose.

My awesome assistant, Eileen, who allows me to interrupt her all day every day. Thanks for your time for typing and for your positive energy.

My Scribe team, Libby, Erin, and especially Janice Bashman, who made sense of my rambling words and kept me on track.

Casey's and Lindsey's encouragement.

Cate's web design and photography.

All of my clients who have trusted me to understand what's important for them.

My incredible family, who make every day spectacular.

MARK CLURE, CFP, is a twenty-five-year veteran financial advisor and a principal at Enso Wealth Management. He is the founder and director of the Financial Guide Service, a Mount Shasta, California,-based training and consulting firm dedicated to empowering potential and creating an ideal life experience. Mark is a serial optimist despite having the tech skills of a four-year-old.

CPSIA information can be obtained
at www.ICGtesting.com
Printed in the USA
LVHW061536060121
675887LV00012B/988